SO YOU THINK YOU'RE A

KENTUCKY WILDCATS BASKETBALL

FAN?

SO YOU THINK YOU'RE A
KENTUCKY
WILDCATS
BASKETBALL
FAN?

STARS, STATS, RECORDS, AND MEMORIES FOR TRUE DIEHARDS

By
TOM WALLACE

SPORTS
PUBLISHING

Sports Publishing books may be purchased in bulk at special discounts for sales promotion, corporate gifts, fund-raising, or educational purposes. Special editions can also be created to specifications. For details, contact the Special Sales Department, Sports Publishing, 307 West 36th Street, 11th Floor, New York, NY 10018 or sportspubbooks@skyhorsepublishing. com.

Sports Publishing® is a registered trademark of Skyhorse Publishing, Inc.®, a Delaware corporation.

Visit our website at www.sportspubbooks.com.

10 9 8 7 6 5 4 3 2 1

Library of Congress Cataloging-in-Publication Data is available on file.

Cover design by Tom Lau
Cover photo: AP Images

ISBN: 978-1-61321-972-0

Ebook ISBN: 978-1-61321-973-7

Printed in the United States of America

Contents

Introduction

OK, so you think you know all there is to know about University of Kentucky basketball. You claim this knowledge because you are a member in good standing of Big Blue Nation, either a lifelong veteran or a relative newcomer. Well, let's find out just how enlightened you are when it comes to Wildcat hoops history. Get ready to be tested to the max.

The primary goal here is to have some fun and to maybe learn a little something along the way. You know, pick up enough information so that one day you can win a few bucks from some know-it-all who actually knows much less than you do. Knocking someone like that off his pedestal is always fun, isn't it?

Our little Wildcat "test" will feature 125 questions that are divided into four different classes, with the degree of difficulty rising with each classification. The classes will be: Benchwarmer, Starter, All-American, and Hall of Fame.

There will be 45 questions for the Benchwarmer section, 40 for Starter, 25 for All-American, and

15 for Hall of Fame. Answers will be found at the end of each section, along with explanations, comments, and a few tall tales.

The 45 Benchwarmer questions are the easiest. If you fail to score at least 90 percent in this category, you will forever be buried at the end of the bench, one seat ahead of the team managers. In short, you won't see much playing time.

Although degree of difficulty will increase with each of the next two categories, you should be able to score 85 percent or better. If you can perform that well, then you have a real shot at being a Wildcats trivia expert.

But the true test of the depth of your Big Blue knowledge will be uncovered in those 15 Hall of Fame questions. There, if you can manage to score 80 percent or better, you can rightfully claim your place as a Wildcats Trivia Legend.

So, do you have your thinking cap on, and are you focused on the task at hand? If you are, then let's begin. It's time to find out where you stand when it comes to Wildcats trivia.

Before I send you on this quest to demonstrate your UK Wildcats expertise, there are a few folks I need to thank for their contribution to this book. Several of them are no longer with us, but that doesn't matter. Their spirit infuses every page of what you are about to read. Without them, this book would not have been possible.

First and foremost, there is Cawood Ledford, a man I had the grand privilege of getting to know up close and personal while working as editor/writer for *Cawood on Kentucky*, his weekly publication covering the Wildcats. Spending nearly eight years with him, working side by side on a daily basis, was like attending a graduate class in UK history. Every day, I had the good fortune to listen to the Master.

Cawood was a terrific storyteller and, boy, could he tell some great ones. He told them about Adolph Rupp, Harry Lancaster, Joe B. Hall, Bernie Shively. There were tall tales about UK players and opposing coaches. And there were stories about other wonderful and colorful characters like Happy Chandler and Al McGuire.

Cawood's autobiography, *Hello Everybody, This is Cawood Ledford*, which he wrote with award-winning sportswriter Billy Reed, was another great source of information for this book.

Another book Billy was heavily involved in, *100 Years of Kentucky Basketball*, which was published by Host Communications, also contained some really good stuff.

Finally, Russell Rice's classic *Big Blue Machine* was extremely helpful. No surprise there. All of us who write about UK's basketball history are venturing into territory Russell staked out many years ago. We all owe him for his groundbreaking work.

For the vast amount of information passed along by Cawood and Russell, two giants who are no longer with us, and Billy, I owe a huge debt of gratitude.

The folks at the UK sports information department have always been generous and helpful any time I've sought their assistance. They've been quick to provide information and access to photos, and for that I am very grateful.

C. M. Newton shared one terrific story with me, as did Rodger Bird, an old buddy from my days as sports editor of the Henderson *Gleaner*. Thanks to both of them.

Most of the photos in this book are courtesy of UK's sports information department. Others are by David Coyle and Team Coyle.

Lastly, let me say that any mistakes or inaccuracies found in this book are solely my own. The buck (blame) stops with me.

Enjoy.

1

BENCHWARMER LEVEL

(Answers begin on Page 7)

1. Let's begin with the most basic question of all: Who is the all-time leading scorer in University of Kentucky basketball history?

2. Name the players known as the "Fabulous Five."

3. Who was "Mr. Outside" to Cotton Nash's "Mr. Inside"?

4. Who were the three players Adolph Rupp dubbed the "Katzenjammer Kids"?

5. Which of these former Wildcats is not a southpaw: Mickey Gibson, Kevin Grevey, Tom Parker, James Lee, Tayshaun Prince, Julius Randle?

6. What UK graduate is the team's most recognizable fan? A hint: she's an actor.

7. What two ex-Cats are the all-time leading scorers in the old American Basketball Association?

8. Pete Maravich scored 312 points in six games against UK. How many of those games did Pistol Pete's LSU Tigers win?

9. Name the starters on the "Fiddlin' Five."

10. Rick Pitino left UK to coach what NBA team?

11. How many games did Adolph Rupp win during his 42-year tenure at UK?

12. Who was famous for giving an emotional rendering of "My Old Kentucky Home" prior to UK home games?

13. What UK team was known as the "Wildkittens"?

14. Who was the first UK player to be selected first overall in the NBA draft?

15. Who were the starters on the beloved "Rupp's Runts" squad?

16. Who succeeded the legendary Cawood Ledford as "Voice of the Wildcats"?

17. What inside duo was known as "King" and "Kong"?

18. Name the Wildcat who was injured in an automobile accident during the summer prior to the 1969–70 season.

19. What team snapped UK's 129-game home-court winning streak in 1955?

For these next ten questions, let's borrow those majestic words found in the Book of Exodus: "I Am That I Am." Identify these guys:

20. I am the former UK All-American who later came back to coach the Wildcats.

21. I am the only Wildcat player to average 20 points per game for three successive seasons.

22. I am the player who ended the 1978 title-game win over Duke by slamming down a thunderous dunk.

23. I am the Wildcat who hit last-second buckets to twice beat Temple during the 1957–58 season.

24. I am the UK player who drew three quick fouls on the great Elgin Baylor during our 1958 title-game win over Seattle.

25. I am the Wildcat from Maysville who was named SEC tourney MVP in 2011.

26. I am the ex-Wildcat who was chosen ahead of Michael Jordan in the 1984 NBA draft.

27. I am the Wildcat who was All-SEC in basketball and football.

28. I am the only Wildcat to record a triple-double.

29. I am the first Wildcat to score 40 points in Rupp Arena.

30. Who is the first—and only—female hired as an assistant coach for the men's team?

31. Which Wildcat was the fastest to reach the 1,000-point mark?

32. What Wildcat broke Dan Issel's record for most points in a game?

33. This guy was a freshman with Pat Riley and Louie Dampier before transferring to Western Kentucky University prior to his sophomore season. Who is he? A hint: His son later played for UK.

34. Who is the former Wildcat who was a 6'0" high school freshman who grew into a 6'10" high school senior?

35. What UK superstar followed the same ritual prior to shooting every free throw?

36. What injured Wildcat came off the bench to hit a pair of free throws during 1997 Final Four semifinal game?

37. Adolph Rupp was notorious for wearing the same color suit at UK games. What was the color?

38. What West Virginia prep standout was Billy Gillispie's first important recruit?

39. Who is the only UK coach to win a national title in his first year on the job?

40. Who was the first Wildcat to score 50 points in a game?

These next five questions are True or False. Pay close attention.

41. Adolph Rupp played college hoops at Kansas State University.

42. UK lost the first game it ever played.

43. Tubby Smith's first name is Oscar.

44. Ex-Cat Lee Huber was a two-time high school tennis champ at Louisville St. Xavier.

45. Jim Master holds the UK record for most consecutive free throws made.

BENCHWARMER ANSWERS

1. OK, I'll admit that this was a trick question. If your answer was Dan Issel, you were wrong. Big Dan scored 2,138 points during his three years as a Wildcat, but the all-time leader is Valerie Still. She tallied 2,763 points during her four years at UK.

   Remember, gender was not mentioned in the question. This is a great question to spring on those folks who think they know more Wildcat trivia than they actually do. You can win some bucks with this one.

   Although Issel would surpass Cotton Nash as UK's all-time leading scorer, he only became a Wildcat after two top prospects— George Janky and Dick Broderson—turned down scholarship offers. Assistant coach Joe B. Hall, who was in charge of recruiting, then set his sights on Issel, who had already signed a National Letter of Intent with the University of Wisconsin. Fortunately for UK fans, Big

Dan changed his mind, pulled out of the deal with Wisconsin, inked his scholarship and became a Wildcat, thus joining Mike Casey and Mike Pratt in one of the school's best recruiting hauls.

As a sophomore, Issel averaged 16.4 points per game (second to Casey's 20.1). It was during his junior year that he became a scoring machine, averaging 26.6 that season, followed by a 33.9 average as a senior. He scored more than 50 points twice, while topping the 40-point mark on seven other occasions.

As for Valerie Still, she is to the women's program what Issel was to the men's. In addition to her point total, she also pulled down 1,525 rebounds. More important, during that span the Wildcats had a record of 96–24. After graduating, she played 12 years in Italy. Her brother Art is arguably UK's all-time greatest football player. He earned All-America honors at UK, then went on to have an All-Pro career in the NFL.

2. Kenny Rollins, Cliff Barker, Wah Wah Jones, Alex Groza, and Ralph Beard. If you didn't know the answer to this question you are relegated to a seat at the back of the class. True Big Blue fans learn the names of these five guys before they learn the US presidents.

    Fate played a big role in the formation of this team. Three players—Barker, Rollins, and Groza—all migrated back to UK after serving in the military. Also, because so many players had been away serving their country, a critical rule change was made—a player could play varsity ball for four years instead of three. That's why Beard and Jones, who came to UK at exactly the right time, were able to play as freshmen in 1945–46.

Here's another little tidbit you might not know: During that 1947–48 season, the Fabulous Five did not become the starting quintet until the Cats played Miami (Ohio) on January 5, 1948, the 12th game of the year. Beard, Groza, and Rollins were starters all along, while Jones had to earn his starting spot after working out the football kinks. It was only when Adolph Rupp inserted the clever Barker into the forward position opposite Jones that the celebrated unit finally came together.

UK's program soared to a new level with the arrival of freshmen Beard and Jones in 1945. During the four years those guys wore the blue and white, UK was virtually unbeatable, carving out a 130–10 record overall, 55–0 against SEC competition, and had a winning margin of 28 points per game.

The cheetah-quick Beard was a burner, a guy who was perpetual motion personified. And, man, was he competitive. He hated to lose. Once, when a sportswriter praised that 130–10 record, Beard's response was, "We should have been 140 and zero."

Jones was the team's enforcer, and no one dared mess with him. One exuberant fan, dressed in a shirt and bow tie, made the mistake of getting in Jones's face after a game. Whatever the guy said, he shouldn't have, because, according to Beard, "Wah grabbed the guy's shirt and decked him with one punch. The guy was on the floor, and Wah was standing over him holding the poor guy's tie and the front of his shirt in his hand."

Adolph Rupp had several really strong teams during his early tenure at UK, but nothing like the ones he had during the Jones-Beard years. It was the beginning of UK's first true "Golden Era."

3. Larry Pursiful. During the 1961–62 season, Pursiful was a senior guard, while Nash was only a sophomore. Those two were big reasons why this surprising Wildcat club finished with a 23–3 record, was ranked No. 3 in the national polls and was co-champions of the Southeastern Conference. Nash, who earned All-America recognition, led the team in scoring with a 23.4 average.

Because Nash was so gifted and such a prolific scorer, the top priority for opposing defenses was to shut him down. Regardless of the foe, Nash was always the center of their attention. To beat the Wildcats they needed to hold him in check, a task not many teams could achieve.

Naturally, those schools wanted to double- or even triple-team Nash. However, Pursiful, a 6'1" guard, was such a deadly outside shooter— he averaged 19.1 points per game as a senior— defenses quickly learned they had to keep him on their radar. Fearing that Pursiful would burn them from long range, they had to pay attention to him, which helped open things up inside for Nash to work his magic.

When making a list of UK's all-time best outside shooters, Pursiful's name has to be included. Rarely has UK had a better or a more lethal inside/outside duo than Cotton Nash and Larry Pursiful.

4. Larry Conley, Tommy Kron, and Mickey Gibson. This talented trio came to UK as freshmen in 1962–63. Conley, from Ashland, and Kron, from Tell City, Indiana, had great careers at UK, and were key members of the Rupp's Runts squad that lost to Texas Western in the 1966 NCAA title game.

Conley had the most immediate impact, earning a starting nod as a sophomore on the 1963–64 team led by senior Cotton Nash. Conley ranks among the most intelligent Wildcats ever, and is without question the finest passer in school history. If a teammate was open, Conley would get him the ball. Nash and Ted Deeken were the chief beneficiaries of Conley's deft passing ability and his unselfish attitude.

Kron made his first start late in his sophomore season in a game that marked the first time one of Rupp's teams employed a zone defense. In a must-win game against Tennessee, UK played what was essentially a 1-3-1 zone with Kron on top.

Rupp, however, refused to admit that his team used something so reprehensible as a zone defense, saying with a straight face that it was "a hyperbolic transitional stratified parabola."

Kron went on to become a full-time starter during the next two seasons, averaging 12.3 points as a junior and 10.2 as a senior.

Unfortunately, Gibson's story had a different ending. The high-jumping 6'2" forward from Hazard was dismissed from the team for disciplinary reasons midway through his sophomore season. His absence hurt, because he was a player who could score, rebound, and defend.

Gibson missed the early part of the season due to academic problems, and didn't make his first appearance until UK beat Wisconsin 108–85 in the opening round of the UKIT. He had nine points in his debut performance.

Gibson's best game was a 19-point effort in a loss at Vanderbilt. In that game, Gibson had one eye-popping moment when he soared above everyone to slam down a dunk.

But when the team departed for Minneapolis to open NCAA tourney action, Gibson was not among those making the trip. Rupp had kicked him off the team, ending what could have been a superb career.

5.   None. This was yet another trick question designed to find out if you are really paying attention and not beginning to nod off. All six

were lefties, with Grevey, Parker, and Prince being the deadliest from long range. Gibson, Lee, and Randle were power players who did their best work closer to the bucket.

6. Ashley Judd, who else? And she's no fly-by-night fan, either. She's hard-core, and she knows the game of basketball. She can talk X's and O's like a coach. That should come as no surprise, because first and foremost she is one very intelligent lady.

Ashley graduated from UK with a major in French, and she didn't just squeak by; she graduated in UK's Honors Program. More recently, she returned to school, receiving an MPA from Harvard's Kennedy School of Government.

She has appeared in many movies and several Broadway productions. Her big-screen break came in the movie *Ruby in Paradise*. Along the way, she more than held her own against such powerful actors as Robert De Niro, Morgan Freeman, and Tommy Lee Jones.

Ashley is true humanitarian, advocate, and activist who is always willing to stand front and center in her effort to support and improve programs dealing with such worldwide issues as poverty, public health, human rights, and social justice. Not a shabby résumé, is it?

UK has to be proud to have her as an alumnus.

This famous actor can talk basketball X's and O's like a coach.
Photo courtesy of University of Kentucky Athletics.

7. Louie Dampier and Dan Issel. During their days
    in the old ABA, Little Louie racked up 13,726
    points, ranking him No. 1, while Big Dan
    accounted for 12,823, good enough for No. 2.
       Those two, along with Artis Gilmore,
    led the Kentucky Colonels to the 1975 ABA
    championship. That club, coached by Hubie
    Brown, finished with a 58–26 regular-season
    record.
       After beating the New York Nets is a one-
    game tiebreaker, the Colonels then stormed
    through the next three series, going 4–1 against
    the Memphis Sounds, the Spirits of St. Louis, and
    the Indiana Pacers.
       For the year, Gilmore was the leading scorer
    with an average of 23.6. Issel was next at 17.7,
    followed by Dampier at 16.8.
       Issel, who went on to have a long stint in the
    NBA, finished his pro career with more than
    27,000 points. Both Issel and Dampier are in the
    Basketball Hall of Fame.

8. None. Despite racking up those 312 points,
    including 64 in one game, Pistol Pete's Tigers
    never did defeat the Wildcats. Perhaps that's
    because defense was a foreign concept to the
    Tigers. The proof: The Wildcats cracked the
    century mark in all six of those high-scoring
    outings. The final scores were: 121–95, 109–96,
    108–96, 103–89, 109–96, and 121–105.
       In addition to his 64-point performance (the
    most ever scored by a UK opponent), Maravich

had games of 52, 44, 52, 45, and 55. Folks, that's an average of 52 points per game. That's a bunch of points.

UK's great Dan Issel didn't exactly run away and hide during those six battles. He scored 185 points against the Tigers.

In the game in which Maravich scored 64 points, Issel had 51. Think about that. In one game those two guys scored more points than many teams do today. That's with no shot clock and no three-point bucket. Count on one thing: we'll never see numbers like that again.

Even though Pistol Pete was the top-scoring opponent, there were many others who shredded UK's defense, including Alabama's Jerry Harper (37), Mississippi State's Bailey Howell (37), West Virginia's Jerry West (36), Ohio State's Jerry Lucas (34), North Carolina's Billy Cunningham (32), Notre Dame's Austin Carr (52), Western Kentucky's Jim McDaniels (35), and LSU's Chris Jackson (41), just to name a few.

9. Vernon Hatton, Ed Beck, Johnny Crigler, Adrian Smith, and Johnny Cox. This quintet, along with solid six-man performances from Don Mills, earned UK its fourth national championship by beating Seattle 84–72 in the title game. Hatton scored 30 points in that victory, with Cox adding 24 and Crigler 14. This would be the last of Adolph Rupp's four NCAA championship teams.

This was not a great UK club. In fact, you could make a strong argument that it is the weakest among UK's eight national championship teams. These Cats had six losses heading into NCAA Tournament action.

Prior to the season, Adolph Rupp said, "We're fiddlers, that's all. They're pretty good fiddlers— be right entertaining at a barn dance. But I'll tell you, you need violinists to play at Carnegie Hall. We don't have any violinists."

But a couple of things happened that increased this team's chances of succeeding in tournament play. First, to this team's credit, the Wildcats played their best basketball when it counted the most. Second, by a stroke of luck, the Cats did not have to travel out of state for any of their games. The first two rounds were played at Memorial Coliseum, the final two rounds at Louisville's Freedom Hall.

Playing well, the Cats destroyed Miami (Ohio) 94–70 and Notre Dame 89–56 to advance to the Final Four. There, they edged Temple 61–60, and then beat Seattle in that title game.

At the postseason banquet, Rupp said, "These boys still are just a bunch of barnyard fiddlers, but they sure can fiddle!"

10. Boston Celtics. Many Louisville haters apparently continue to live with the misguided belief that Rick Pitino is a traitor for having traded his UK blue for U of L red. In their revisionist history,

Pitino scorned the Cats to take over the reins at Louisville.

Not true, of course. In between those two jobs, Pitino had a relatively brief and unsuccessful stop in Beantown as head man for the Celtics. It was only after leaving Boston that Pitino signed on as Louisville's coach.

Why UK fans have such a negative opinion of Pitino is somewhat baffling given what he did for a basketball program that was reeling from a scandal and coming off the first losing season in sixty-one years. *Sports Illustrated* had a cover that read "Kentucky's Shame." Those were bleak times for UK and for Big Blue Nation.

Before Pitino's first season got under way, Cawood Ledford told him, "Rick, if you win ten games this season, you should be National Coach of the Year."

Well, Pitino's first club, consisting of a bunch of gutsy young players no one had much faith in, managed to break even with a 14–14 record. His second team, though still not eligible to participate in the NCAA tourney, had a 22–6 record overall and a league-best 14–4 mark in SEC play.

Over the next six seasons, three UK teams made it to the Final Four, with the 1995–96 club taking home all the marbles. And were it not for an injury to Derek Anderson, UK likely would have repeated in 1996–97.

The success Tubby Smith and John Calipari have enjoyed at UK would not have been possible

Adolph Rupp diagrams a play.
Photo courtesy of University of Kentucky Athletics.

had Pitino failed to turn "Kentucky's Shame" into "Kentucky's Pride."

11. During his long and magnificent career, Adolph Rupp's overall record was 876–190, a winning percentage of .822. His teams won four NCAA championships, one NIT title, and 27 Southeastern Conference crowns.

In addition to those achievements, Rupp helped coach the 1948 Olympic team to a gold medal in London. That team included Wildcats Alex Groza, Ralph Beard, Kenny Rollins, Wah Wah Jones, and Cliff Barker.

From his earliest days at UK, Rupp was a shrewd operator. He was also a coach with lofty goals. Rupp had little desire for UK to become simply the best team in the South. No, he wanted UK to be viewed as a big player on the national stage.

That's why, early on, Rupp took teams to New York City, Chicago, Cincinnati, Omaha, New Orleans, and Long Island. His teams and his players were given national exposure, which helped cement UK's reputation as a top-notch basketball school.

There is simply no denying the fact that Rupp, the Baron of the Bluegrass, is the father of UK basketball. He is also the man who almost single-handedly made basketball popular in the football-mad South.

Rupp died on December 11, 1977, at the age of seventy-six.

Happy Chandler with Fiddlers Ed Beck, Johnny Cox, Vernon Hatton, Johnny Crigler, and Adrian Smith.
Photo courtesy of University of Kentucky Athletics.

12. Happy Chandler. When the former Kentucky governor and ex-baseball commissioner sang "My Old Kentucky Home" prior to a UK game, you would be hard-pressed to find a dry eye in Rupp Arena.

Chandler, a close friend and confidant to Adolph Rupp, often attended UK's practices, which were notoriously famous for the sacred silence. Balls bouncing and sneakers squeaking were the only sounds Rupp wanted to hear, or would tolerate hearing. Among Rupp's most famous lines was one he often uttered at practice: "Don't speak unless you can improve the silence."

At one practice, when the players were not performing well, Rupp raised his head and hands and prayed, "Dear God, would you please send me someone who is worth a damn?" Immediately, Chandler appeared, prompting Rupp to say, "Thank you, God."

However, moments later, Chandler, a nonstop talker, committed the ultimate transgression by shattering the silence. An angry Rupp turned to his buddy and sternly said, "I don't care if you are the governor, either shut up or get out." Chandler was silent for the remainder of practice.

Without question, though, Chandler's greatest accomplishment came when he went against fifteen major league team owners and sided with Branch Rickey in his quest to break the color barrier by signing Jackie Robinson to a Brooklyn Dodgers contract. This was absolutely unthinkable at the time.

Chandler's reasoning was simple: Knowing many black soldiers died during World War II, Chandler said, "When I meet my Maker, and He asks me why I didn't allow Robinson to play, what excuse could I possibly give that would satisfy Him?"

13. The 1943–44 team was given this moniker for the simple reason that its roster was filled with extremely young and inexperienced players.

Until our current era, in which so many freshmen are playing, this was probably UK's youngest team ever. Adolph Rupp said coaching this team was like running a kindergarten. He sometimes referred to this gang of juveniles as "Beardless Wonders."

Remember, this was smack in the middle of the World War II years. A player might get drafted, or he might leave school to join in the fight. An opening-game roster could have a totally different look by the end of the season.

Kenny Rollins is a perfect example. He came to UK in 1941, and was a sophomore starter during the 1942–43 campaign. He didn't graduate from UK until 1948, after returning from the war.

When this season opened, UK's roster consisted of fifteen freshmen and two sophomores. Despite the youth and inexperience, this team managed a 19–2 record, won the SEC Tournament, and came in third in the NIT, then a far tougher and far more prestigious event than the NCAA tourney.

The key to this team's success was the play of center Bob Brannum, who averaged 12.1 points per game, good enough to earn him All-America recognition. Other starters on this team were sophomores Wilbur Schu and Tom Moseley, the club's two "senior citizens," and freshmen Jack Tingle and Jack Parkinson.

Despite its sterling record—and big wins over Ohio State, St. John's, and Notre Dame—it's difficult to know where to rank this team among UK's all-time best. Due to restrictions on travel during the war, UK did not play a regular-season SEC schedule. In fact, this team didn't meet any SEC foes until tournament time.

Not having to play in such hostile environments as Knoxville, Tuscaloosa, Baton Rouge, Starkville, and Auburn makes it virtually impossible to know just how good this team might have been.

14. John Wall. In his only season as a Wildcat, Wall, a 6'4" guard with blazing speed, scored at a 16.6 clip while handing out 241 assists, including 16 in a win over Hartford. Wall was drafted by the Washington Wizards. From baseline to baseline, with ball in hand, he may have been the fastest Wildcat ever.

Wall also created something of a sensation when he came up with the "John Wall Dance." He's another one of those guys you wish could have stayed around for two or three years. He was fun to watch.

After Wall, two other Wildcats have since been drafted first overall—Anthony Davis (New Orleans) and Karl-Anthony Towns (Minnesota).

The exciting John Wall had more than enough talent to make John Calipari smile.
Photo courtesy of University of Kentucky Athletics.

The 1965–66 Wildcats included, sitting (l-r): Adolph Rupp, Gene Stewart, Pat Riley, Louie Dampier, Bobby Tallent, Steve Clevenger, Jim LeMaster, and Harry Lancaster. Standing (l-r): Tommy Porter, Gary Gamble, Tommy Kron, Cliff Berger, Larry Lentz, Brad Bounds, Thad Jaracz, Larry Conley, and manager Mike Harreld.
Photo courtesy of University of Kentucky Athletics.

15. Larry Conley, Tommy Kron, Pat Riley, Louie Dampier, and Thad Jaracz. This is yet another one of those "must-know" answers that should be permanently stored away in your memory bank if you having any hope of being considered a true Big Blue trivia expert.

This 1965–66 club ranks among most UK fans' all-time favorites, and for good reason. Despite being a small team—Kron, a 6'5" guard, was the tallest starter—this bunch could get up and down the court, and they could shoot the lights out. That's especially true of Dampier and Riley, both of whom were lethal shooters.

And thanks to the unselfishness of seniors Conley and Kron, who willingly sacrificed personal glory for the good of the team, the on-court chemistry was off the charts.

Though it's virtually impossible to imagine now, when that season got under way no one expected much from this team. Four starters were returning from a very mediocre team that had a less-than-outstanding 15–10 record the previous season.

But this team showed early on that this was not going to be a repeat of last year, as the Cats won their first 23 games before losing at Tennessee.

One critical component of this team's success that too often gets lost in the sound of all the hosannas heaped upon the starting five is a solid group of substitutes. Cliff Berger, Bobby Tallent, Gary Gamble, Tommy Porter, Jim LeMaster, Steve Clevenger, Gene Stewart, Larry Lentz, and Brad Bounds all had moments when their contributions made the difference between winning and losing.

Few UK teams have ever been more fun to watch. This team posted a 27–2 record, won the SEC title, and finished as runner-up to Texas Western in the 1966 NCAA tourney.

16. Ralph Hacker. After serving as Cawood's sidekick for twenty years, Hacker had the difficult task of following his mentor as the "Voice of the Wildcats" in 1992. That's akin to the guy who had to follow Adolph Rupp at Kentucky or John Wooden at UCLA. Following a legend is no simple thing. Ask Joe B. Hall or Gene Bartow if you have any doubts.

Hacker served nine years as "Voice of the Wildcats," meaning he spent a total of twenty-nine years as part of the University of Kentucky Radio Network. In addition to his basketball duties, he spent five years as the UK football play-by-play guy.

Hacker, a Richmond native, began his broadcasting career at the age of fifteen, doing high school games. One year later, he was calling football and basketball games for Eastern Kentucky University. He would go on to have a hugely successful career in radio.

When Hacker decided to step down after the 2000–01 season, he turned the microphone over to Tom Leach.

17. Rick Robey and Mike Phillips. Both were big, strong inside players who were not afraid of a little contact. In fact, it's more accurate to say they kind of preferred it when things got rough. These two were not exactly shrinking violets.

They played from 1975–78, helping lead UK to the NIT title in 1976 and the NCAA championship in 1978. In that 94–88 championship-game win over Duke, Robey had 20 points and 11 rebounds. Of course, that game belonged to Jack Givens, who poured in 41 points.

Two years earlier, with Robey sidelined by an injury, Phillips came up big in UK's 71–67 win over UNC-Charlotte in the 1976 NIT final. In that game, Phillips accounted for 16 points and seven rebounds.

During their time at UK, both scored more than 1,000 points—Robey had 1,395, Phillips had 1,367. Robey also pulled down 838

Adolph Rupp with Mike Casey, Dan Issel, and Mike Pratt.
Photo courtesy of University of Kentucky Athletics.

rebounds, while Phillips once snared 28 missed shots against Tennessee.

Robey and Phillips were also referred to as the "Twin Towers," a moniker later applied to the tandem of Sam Bowie and Melvin Turpin.

18. Mike Casey. The tough-minded Casey, who came to UK in a freshman class that also included Dan Issel and Mike Pratt, suffered a badly broken leg that sidelined him for the 1969–70 campaign. This was a tremendous loss, one that cast a pall over the entire season.

Upon hearing about Casey's serious injury, Adolph Rupp said, "Well, there goes the national championship." Rupp may have been right, too. With Casey, Issel, and Pratt back for their senior year, the Cats did stand an excellent chance of winning it all. Not having Casey was a killer.

Casey, a Shelby County High grad, wasted no time showing just how good he was, racking up 28 points in his first varsity game. A few weeks later he flashed his you-can't-beat-me attitude by turning in a splendid 27-point, six-steal performance in a come-from-behind 81–73 victory over Notre Dame at Freedom Hall.

Little wonder that Rupp once tabbed Casey as "the best money player I ever had."

Casey did come back to play during the 1970–71 campaign, and though he acquitted himself well he was not the same player he was before the injury. He ended his career with 1,535 points. In all, the Casey-Issel-Pratt trio combined to score 5,032 for the Wildcats.

19. Georgia Tech. On a night when the Cats were expected to win easily, the visiting Yellow Jackets shocked the basketball world by pulling off an improbable 59–58 upset.

When the final horn sounded, most Wildcat fans, virtually all of whom had *never* seen UK lose a game, sat for a long time in stunned silence. Remember, UK had not lost a home game since January 2, 1943. Only after a few minutes had passed and the shock had begun to sink in did the fans begin to exit Memorial Coliseum.

Georgia Tech was of so little concern that the UK coaches barely scouted them. Cawood Ledford later said that a few hours before the game, he and his color man, Paul Cowley, were having a bowl of chili and talking about the UK subs, because they didn't think the starters were going to play very much that night.

Well, that overconfidence proved to be the downfall for the Wildcats. Georgia Tech led 26–23 at intermission, then expanded the lead to 38–30. Minutes later, a bucket by Phil Grawemeyer capped an 8–0 run that had the Cats on top 52–46.

But on this night the Cats couldn't stand prosperity.

The Yellow Jackets rallied, hitting four free throws and a field goal to draw even with just under five minutes remaining. After Linville

Puckett scored for UK, Joe Helms hit one of two freebies and Dick Lenholt added two more to give Tech a 55–54 lead.

Bob Burrow and Grawemeyer combined for four unanswered points to put the Cats in front 58–55, but then Tech's Bobby Kimmel canned two free tosses to make it 58–57 with 1:12 left to play.

Then with 24 ticks remaining, following a jump ball in which UK gained possession, Helms moved in, swiped the ball from Billy Evans, and nailed the game-winner. The Cats had two final chances to pull out the win, but a Puckett jumper and a tip-in attempt by Grawemeyer both missed their mark. This one belonged to the Yellow Jackets.

Following the setback, Adolph Rupp told his players, "From this time until history is no longer recorded, you will be remembered as the team that broke the string. Even if you go on to win the NCAA championship, you must carry this scar with you for the rest of your lives."

Rupp would later claim that the two worst disasters in his lifetime were Pearl Harbor and this loss to Georgia Tech. Perhaps Rupp and those UK fans shouldn't have been so shocked, because it happened a second time. Later that season Georgia Tech did it again, beating the Cats 65–59 in Atlanta.

Here are the answers to the ten "I Am" questions:

20. Basil Hayden. He holds the distinction of being UK's first All-American player, earning that honor in 1921. He was an outstanding all-around athlete known for his defense and rebounding.

UK claimed its first championship in 1921, winning the Southern Intercollegiate Athletic Association Tournament. In the final game, a 20–19 upset of favored Georgia, Hayden's bucket knotted the score at 19–19.

Hayden later returned to his alma mater and held the head coaching position for one season—1926–27. Hayden's year at the top was not successful as his Wildcats finished with a dismal 3–13 record. This was UK's last losing season until the 1988–89 club went 13–19.

21. Cotton Nash. He averaged 23.4 as a sophomore, 20.6 during an injury-plagued junior season, and 24.0 as a senior. UK was slumping somewhat when Nash arrived on the scene, both on the court and in the eyes of many fans. On the heels of back-to-back mediocre seasons, UK was no longer at the top of the basketball world.

The reason for UK's downslide was simple: lack of talent. Over the previous few years, Adolph Rupp and assistant coach Harry Lancaster didn't have much luck on the recruiting trail. Several terrific players signed with UK, then for various reasons either didn't show up, or did show up but didn't hang around very long.

During this time frame, UK also missed out on two marvelous in-state talents—Lexington

Lafayette's Jeff Mullins, who went to Duke, and Louisville St. Xavier's Mike Silliman, who ended up at Army. What this meant was that after Johnny Cox graduated, the Cats had some decent players, but certainly none that could be regarded as superstars.

That changed when Nash showed up. Instantly, Rupp had a super-talented player to build around. And Nash's impact was immediate. That 1961–62 club finished with a 23–3 record,

Cotton Nash was a three-time All-American and one of the most gifted players to wear a UK uniform.

Photo courtesy of University of Kentucky Athletics.

Nash averaged 23.4 points, and the Cats were SEC co-champs.

Such was Nash's popularity that it was during his time at UK that season ticket sales skyrocketed. And in 1964, UK earned a No. 1 ranking for the first time since 1959.

His popularity and his success on the court prompted Cawood Ledford to write that, "as far as I'm concerned, they ought to build a monument to the guy. He literally carried the program on his back for three years."

Nash was also a superb baseball player, and is one of only a handful of athletes who played both major league baseball and pro basketball.

22. James Lee. The Cats' 94–88 championship win over Duke was signed, sealed, and delivered when Lee jammed in one of his patented dunks just ahead of the final horn. Lee's exciting throw-downs were nothing new to Wildcat fans, who had watched him do it for four years. But the timing made this one something special, because it came on college basketball's biggest stage.

In that title tilt, the Cats, with red-hot Jack Givens and Rick Robey leading the way, built a comfortable lead, and were safely on top with just over a minute to play. That's when Joe B. Hall pulled his starters from the game, a move that almost turned into a disaster. Duke sliced the difference to four points—92–88—when Hall opted to insert the starters back into the game.

With Duke pressing full-court, Lee managed to get behind the defense, haul in a long pass, and then take it to the rack with serious intent. His bucket accounted for the final score.

Lee, a former All-State performer at Lexington Henry Clay High School, still ranks as arguably UK's greatest sixth man and one of the school's most exciting players.

23. Vernon Hatton. If it were a crime to shoot down Owls, Hatton would still be behind bars. The Temple Owls would make sure of that. The steel-nerved Hatton gunned down the Owls on two occasions during the 1957–58 campaign, the first time coming when he hit a 47-footer at the end of the first overtime that tied the score, brought about a second OT, and kept his team's hopes alive.

The two teams eventually went into a third overtime before the dust settled and the Owls had their wings clipped. When the final horn sounded, Hatton's Cats survived that epic battle, 85–83.

He scored six of his club's 10 points in the final OT period. But Hatton's heroics began even earlier, when, with 49 seconds left in regulation play, he dropped in a free throw that tied it 65–65 and set the stage for his subsequent dramatics.

The Cats were down 71–69 with three seconds left in the first overtime. Following a UK timeout, Johnny Crigler inbounded the ball to Hatton, who immediately launched his desperation shot. It was dead center, tying the score and saving the Cats from a rare homecourt loss.

Then, in the NCAA Tournament semifinal round, Hatton did it again, scoring on a layup with 16 seconds left to give his team a come-from-behind 61–60 victory.

One night later, the Cats topped Seattle 84–72 to win it all. Performances like those are why Hatton will always rank among UK's all-time greatest clutch performers.

24. Johnny Crigler. Facing a strong Seattle club in the 1958 NCAA title game, the Cats needed to find a way to neutralize the great Elgin Baylor in order to win. They didn't totally succeed—Baylor finished with 25 points and 19 rebounds—but Crigler did manage to draw three quick first-half fouls on the Seattle superstar and a fourth with 16:44 left to play in the second half. At that time, UK was trailing 44–38.

With Baylor forced to play more cautiously, the Cats roared back to claim the big trophy with an 84–72 victory.

The plan to stop Baylor, who had 23 points and 22 rebounds in the semifinal game, came via a stroke of luck. After seeing Baylor in action, just about everyone was in agreement that he might very well be the best basketball player they had ever seen. And make no mistake about it, he was darn good.

After the pregame meal Saturday morning, Rupp and assistant coach Harry Lancaster still hadn't come up with a game plan, so they sent the players back to their hotel rooms. Then the two coaches retreated to Rupp's room in the Seelbach Hotel, where they would address the problem of stopping Baylor.

As they were trying to come up with something that might work, there was a knock on the door. The visitor was John Grayson, the head coach at Idaho State, and he had come to tell them how to beat Seattle.

First, Grayson advised, Rupp had to keep his players from being mesmerized by Baylor, who was so flashy that everyone, fans and opposing players alike, tended to lock in on him and watch his every move. Second, Baylor wasn't a very good defender against a player who liked to drive to the bucket.

Having been handed the keys to the kingdom, Rupp gathered his troops so they could watch some film of Baylor in action. What they saw convinced them that they had found a way to handle the great Elgin Baylor.

More luck came UK's way when the game got started. For whatever reason, Seattle coach John Castellani chose to have Baylor guard Crigler rather than the low-scoring Ed Beck.

The rest is history. While Baylor was forced to play tentatively, Vernon Hatton and Johnny Cox weren't. They combined for 54 points—

Johnny Crigler drives in for an easy two against Temple in NCAA tourney action.
Photo courtesy of University of Kentucky Athletics.

Hatton had 30, Cox 24—and the Cats took home the championship.

Although Crigler was one of the heroes in that Seattle win, he wasn't above catching serious criticism from Rupp. That was certainly the case during a regular-season game against Auburn, when Crigler's man scored the tying bucket right before halftime.

In *Big Blue Machine*, Russell Rice recalled what happened next. In the dressing room, Rupp, in what has to be among the most hilarious critiques ever uttered, said, "John Lloyd, 150 years from now there will be no university, no field house. There will have been an atomic war, and it will all have been destroyed. But underneath the rubble there will be a monument, which will be inscribed, 'Here lies John Lloyd Crigler, the most stupid basketball player ever at Kentucky, killed by Adolph Rupp,' because, boy, if you don't play better, I'm going to kill you."

Only Adolph Rupp could come up with something like that.

25. Darius Miller. The Maysville native and Mason County High School graduate was a solid, productive performer during his four-year career at UK. In 2011, after giving several superb performances, he was named the SEC tourney's Most Valuable Player.

Later, when the 2012 NCAA championship team visited the White House, Miller was chosen to present president Barack Obama with a UK jersey.

Miller was named Kentucky's Mr. Basketball after leading Mason County to the 2008 state title. He averaged 19.9 points per game that season.

Miller scored 1,248 points during his time as a Wildcat. He was also a member of the US gold medal-winning team in the U-19 World Championships played in New Zealand.

26. Sam Bowie. He was the second pick in the 1984 NBA draft, sandwiched between Hakeem Olajuwon (Houston) and Michael Jordan (Chicago). There is no doubt that Bowie very well might have been the first overall pick had he not missed two seasons due to a leg injury.

    Few seven-footers before or since were more agile and versatile than Bowie. He could score down low and he had a nice soft mid-range jumper. Despite rarely playing at full strength, he still managed to score 1,285 points, pull down 843 rebounds, and shoot 52.2 percent from the field.

    Bowie averaged 12.9 points as a freshman and 17.4 as a sophomore. Then because of injuries, he missed the next two seasons. After the lengthy layoff, he returned for the 1983–84 campaign and scored at a 10.5 clip.

    Injuries would also dampen what should have been a terrific NBA career. He did manage to play ten seasons as a pro, ending his career with a 10.9 scoring average.

Bowie will always be one of those big "what ifs" in the world of college and pro hoops. But of one thing you can be certain: Were it not for his injuries, his being chosen ahead of Jordan might not look so outrageous. Or be the answer to a trivia question.

27. Wallace "Wah Wah" Jones. Arguably, UK's greatest all-around athlete, he was a standout at football, baseball, and basketball while playing for two true icons of college coaching. He scored points and grabbed rebounds for Adolph Rupp, and he hauled in passes and tackled opposing runners for Bear Bryant.

He played on teams that won the Kentucky high school state championship, the NCAA championship (twice), the NIT championship, an Olympic gold medal, and the Great Lakes Bowl. He is the only UK player to have his jersey retired in both basketball and football.

Because Wah Wah played football—the final game was always a Saturday affair against archrival Tennessee—he was behind when it came to basketball conditioning. Therefore, he had to work his way into playing shape. That meant beginning the season as a sub.

But not to worry—it didn't take him long to earn back his starting position. Truth is, that spot was always waiting for him. Adolph Rupp knew it, and so did everyone else. No one or nothing was going to keep him out of the starting lineup.

In the annals of Kentucky sports, high school and college, Wah Wah Jones, a native of Harlan, ranks among the true legends.

28. Chris Mills. Although Mills only played one season at UK—and it was a bleak one in which the scandal-ridden Cats had the school's first losing record in sixty-one seasons—he acquitted himself well, averaging 14.3 points per game. It was against Austin Peay that Mills performed the rare hat trick, scoring 19 points, grabbing 10 rebounds, and dishing out 10 assists.

The talented Mills was at the center of the controversy that led to UK being hit hard by NCAA sanctions. The infamous Emery Air Freight envelope containing $1,000 that popped open was addressed to Mills's father in Los Angeles. Mills was at the time one of the nation's top prep prospects.

After being ruled ineligible to play at UK, Mills transferred to Arizona, where he had an excellent career.

To this day, Mills is the only male Wildcat to manage a triple-double. (Makayla Epps did it for the Lady Wildcats during the 2015–16 season.)

29. Derrick Miller. As backcourt player on Rick Pitino's first UK team, Miller was known for his outside shooting prowess, which he proved against Vanderbilt. In that 100–73 victory,

Miller nailed six second-half treys en route to his 40-point effort.

Miller's outside gunning was one of the reasons why this team, which was noted for launching from long range, was labeled "Pitino's Bombinos." The three-point shot was made for this guy, and he was certainly born to shoot it. And no one ever accused Miller of being shy about firing up those jumpers.

The slender Miller was a senior and the "old man" on Pitino's first team. He led that club in scoring with a 19.2 average. He averaged 13.9 the previous season, Eddie Sutton's last one at UK.

Miller ended his career with 1,156 points.

30. Bernadette Locke-Mattox. She was on the UK coaching staff from 1990 to 1994, having been hired by Rick Pitino. Later, she served eight seasons as head coach for the UK women's program. In 1998, she was an assistant coach for the USA gold medal-winning National Team at the World Championships.

A standout player at the University of Georgia, she was that school's first female athlete to earn both All-America and Academic All-America recognition.

31. Cotton Nash. It only took Nash 45 games to hit the 1,000-point mark, four fewer than it took Dan Issel. He joined that elite club with an unusually low 14-point performance in a 94–71 win over Florida during the 1962–63 season.

Despite playing in just 78 games, Nash scored 1,770 points, which at the time pushed him past Alex Groza as UK's all-time leading scorer. And he did it while consistently being ask to play out of position.

At 6'5", he usually had to operate in the low-post area even though he was certainly capable of going outside to either nail a long-range jumper or use his slick moves to drive past a defender. The fact is he could score from just about anywhere.

But based on his size and athletic ability he would have fit in more naturally as a big guard or a small forward. However, during his years as a Wildcat, he was the tallest starter, which necessitated his playing down low.

Nash currently stands ninth on UK's all-time scoring list.

32. Jodie Meeks. Because today's over-coached college games tend to be defense-minded, low-scoring affairs, there were many who felt that Dan Issel's single-game mark of 53 points would never be surpassed. After all, it was a record that stood for thirty-nine years.

But Meeks shattered it when he erupted for 54 points against Tennessee, making good on 15 of 22 shots from the field, including 10 of 15 behind the three-point line. He also connected on all 14 free throw attempts. It was a singular performance by the 6'4" guard from Norcross,

Georgia, who scored 1,246 points despite playing in only 81 games in a Wildcat uniform.

That record-breaking outburst was the best of several turned in by Meeks. He scored 46 against Appalachian State and 45 against Arkansas. On four other occasions, he topped the 30-point mark.

After posting those numbers, it's not surprising that he earned All-America and All-SEC recognition.

33. Wayne Chapman. Talk about a gifted trio of rookies—the versatile 6'6" Chapman, Louie Dampier, and Pat Riley all averaged more than 20 points per game as freshmen in 1963–64.

All were counted on to be big contributors for the next three seasons. Dampier and Riley fulfilled those expectations, but not Chapman, who left UK and transferred to Western Kentucky after his rookie campaign. His absence was felt immediately—without his size, scoring, rebounding, and athletic ability, the 1964–65 squad could do no better than a mediocre 15–10 record.

One can only wonder what an impact he would have had on that 1965–66 Rupp's Runts team had he remained at UK. No doubt that team would have been even better than it was. Chapman was an exceptionally good basketball player, one who could help a team every way possible.

Chapman had an outstanding career for the Hilltoppers, and was the co-MVP of the Ohio Valley Conference as a senior. His son Rex played two seasons at UK, and remains one of the school's most exciting and popular players.

34. Anthony Davis. One reason why Davis could handle the ball better than most college big men is because he played in the backcourt while growing up. All through his younger years he perfected his ball-handling skills while playing the guard position.

    However, that all changed during high school when he had a sudden and enormous growth spurt that transformed him from a guard to an extremely mobile inside player.

    At UK, Davis was exceptional. He averaged 14.2 points, 10.4 rebounds, shot 62 percent from the field, blocked 186 shots, and recorded 20 double-doubles. He was so dominant that despite scoring only six points in the NCAA title game, he was named the Final Four MVP.

    In truth, Davis was still developing physically while he was at UK. After witnessing what he's done in his young NBA career, it's scary to think how good he might have been had he remained at UK for three or four years. It's not outlandish to argue that he would have been considered the greatest Wildcat of all-time.

35. Kyle Macy. An entire generation of young Kentucky high school players didn't dare attempt a free throw without following Macy's standard

routine of placing his right toe on the nail at the center of the free throw line, bending over and wiping his hands on his socks, and then shadow shooting.

It worked, too. For his career, Macy made good on 89 percent of his charity tosses. The guy known as "Cool Kyle" also had a well-earned reputation for being tough in clutch situations, which he showed by hitting 10 pressure-packed free throws in UK's 52–49 NCAA tourney win over Magic Johnson's Michigan State team.

Macy, the son of a coach, was a true leader on the floor. After transferring to UK from Purdue and sitting out a season, Macy took over as floor general for the powerful 1977–78 team that captured the NCAA title.

During that season, in which the Cats went 30–2, Macy averaged 12.5 points per game. His numbers jumped to 15.2 as a junior and 15.4 as a senior. Twice he earned first-team All-America recognition.

Macy was then, and remains so today, one of Big Blue Nation's most popular players ever.

36. Derek Anderson. This gifted player, who transferred to UK from Ohio State, possessed the blend of quickness, athleticism, offensive ability, and defensive daring that made him the prototypical Rick Pitino–type player.

He averaged 9.4 points as a junior on the talent-rich 1996 NCAA championship team that went 34–2. The next year, he was averaging 18.6

points and was perhaps on his way to an MVP season when he went down with a torn ACL in January. The injury effectively ended his college career.

Not quite. During UK's 78–69 semifinal victory over Minnesota, Pitino sent Anderson into the game to shoot a pair of free throws following a technical on Minnesota coach Clem Haskins. Despite having not played for more than two months, Anderson swished the two freebies.

Two nights later, the Cats lost to Arizona in overtime. Many observers continue to believe that had Anderson been healthy the Cats would have claimed a second consecutive NCAA crown.

37. Brown. One of Adolph Rupp's many nicknames was "the Man in the Brown Suit."

No one is certain when this sartorial tradition started, although legend has it that while coaching at Freeport High in Illinois he lost a game while wearing a blue suit. The next game he wore brown, his team won, and he never changed the routine.

Rupp was a guy who stuck with what was working for him. This included his starting lineup. When his teams were winning, which was often, he rarely made a change to his lineup card.

In fact, Rupp seldom used his subs. Unless a player was injured, ill, or simply stinking the place up, he usually remained in the game. If a

Ermal Allen was a sneaky, wily player.
Photo courtesy of University of Kentucky Athletics.

player did get bumped from the starting quintet and the team continued to win, that guy could easily find himself sitting on the bench for a long time.

So, what was a former starter to do in order to get back in the lineup once he had lost his spot? Be clever (devious?), of course. And no one can accuse wily Ermal Allen of not being clever.

Allen, a decent player back in the early 1940s, was a starting guard until he fell ill, which caused him to miss several games. While he was sidelined, the Cats continued to win, meaning Rupp wasn't going to shake things up. After regaining his health and returning to the team, Allen was now in the dreaded role of substitute.

Allen had to find a way to get back in the starting lineup, and that's exactly what he did. On a bus ride to an away game, Allen just happened to be sitting next to the player who took his place in the lineup. While the guy wasn't looking, Allen reached into his teammate's gym bag, removed his sneakers, and tossed them out the window.

When the team arrived at the gym and the players started dressing for the game, the guy quickly discovered that he had no sneakers. Well, you can't play basketball in your socks, so he had to sit this one out. And who got the nod to replace him? Ermal Allen, of course.

You can make a strong case that this might not have been a kosher thing to do, but it did get Allen back in the starting lineup. Whatever works, right?

38. Patrick Patterson. When Patterson inked his UK scholarship, everyone felt that the Billy Gillispie Era was going to be a roaring success. Didn't happen. Gillispie lasted only two seasons at UK before being fired.

Patterson spent (suffered?) his first two seasons under Gillispie's stern and uneven command, then played his final year for John Calipari. Regardless of what was transpiring behind the scenes, or how uncomfortable things got on and off the court, Patterson proved himself to be among the classiest Wildcats ever. He was a true gentleman from start to finish. And one heckuva basketball player.

He averaged 16.4 as a freshman and 17.9 as a sophomore. Naturally, he was expected to be the big gun as a junior. But when Calipari showed up, he brought John Wall and DeMarcus Cousins with him. Almost immediately, the spotlight shifted away from Patterson and onto his two new teammates.

To his credit, Patterson never once complained or whined about not being the center of attention. All he did was quietly and efficiently go about the business of playing winning basketball.

In his final season, he averaged 14.3 points on a team that finished with a 35–3 record. For his career, Patterson scored 1,564 points and grabbed 791 rebounds.

39. This is ridiculously easy. The answer is Tubby Smith, of course.

After serving on Rick Pitino's staff, and then as head coach at Tulsa and Georgia, the affable Smith came back to take over as UK's head honcho in 1997. And did he start out with a bang!

His first team won 35 games (then the most-ever by a coach in his initial season at the school), claimed the national championship, the SEC crown, and the SEC Tournament title.

For his efforts, Smith was named 1998 National Coach of the Year.

During his 10-year stint, Smith's teams had an overall record of 263–83 for a 76 percent winning clip. While those numbers were good, they weren't good enough for the always-demanding UK fans, who called the coach "10-loss Tubby."

Sensing the rocky marriage was over, Smith resigned and took the head coaching position at the University of Minnesota.

With Smith gone, the UK brain trust brought in Billy Gillispie. And it wouldn't take long before Big Blue Fans were experiencing the feeling of buyer's remorse.

40. Cliff Hagan. He cracked the 50-point mark when he scored 51 in the season opener against Temple on December 5, 1953. Only four Wildcats have scored 50 points in a game—Hagan, Dan Issel (twice), Bob Burrow, and Jodie Meeks.

Hagan's outburst came in UK's first game in nearly two years. Because of UK's involvement in

Adolph Rupp presents the game ball to the magnificent Cliff Hagan.
Photo courtesy of University of Kentucky Athletics.

the point-shaving scandal, the school was banned from playing during 1952–53. All UK could do was practice and have scrimmage games.

So, when Temple came to town, Adolph Rupp had his team primed and ready for action. Stated more accurately, Rupp, who burned at having been sanctioned by the NCAA, had his team ready to gain a measure of revenge against anyone and everyone.

In the opener, UK beat Temple 86–59, the first of 25 wins without a defeat. But because its top three players were graduate students, UK did not participate in the NCAA Tournament.

Had UK done so, and had those three players participated, it's almost a sure thing that the Cats would have won it all. The 1953–54 team surely rates among UK's all-time greatest.

Here are the answers to the True/False questions:

41. False. Adolph Rupp played at the University of Kansas under the guidance of Phog Allen, one of the early giants of college basketball coaching. Rupp graduated from Kansas in 1923. While in school Rupp got to know Dr. James Naismith, the man who invented the game of basketball. Therefore, it is accurate to say that Rupp's basketball roots can be traced back to the inception of the sport.

    There is a terrific photo of the 1923 Kansas team, one in which the youthful Rupp is to the far left on the back row. In the middle row, side by side, are Coach Allen and Dr. Naismith.

    Rupp would later coach against—and beat—his former coach. He would also far surpass Allen's total number of 746 wins.

42. True. On the afternoon of February 6, 1903, UK, the winningest program of all time, lost to Georgetown (Kentucky) College. At the time UK was known as Kentucky State College.

    Also, at the time basketball wasn't viewed as a serious sport. Mainly, it was seen as an activity meant to help keep athletes in shape in the months between the end of football season in the fall and the start of baseball in the spring.

The initial game was of such insufficient interest that the two local newspapers couldn't agree on the final score. The *Herald* had it 17–6, while the *Leader* said it was 15–6. The UK archives credit the 15–6 score as being official. Sadly, the name of the player who scored UK's first points has been lost to time.

UK split its next two games, beating the Lexington YMCA 11–10, then suffering a humbling 42–2 drubbing at the hands of Kentucky University (now Transylvania College).

Despite such an inglorious beginning the sport caught on, and it wasn't long before basketball became *the* big thing in Kentucky.

43. False. No, no, no, everyone knows his name is Orlando. Smith, one of 17 children, led the UK program for 10 years after serving as Rick Pitino's assistant and then spending four years as head coach at Tulsa and two more at Georgia.

    Smith, whose 1998 squad captured the NCAA title, will always be remembered as a man of class and integrity.

44. True. Lee Huber was a set-shot artist who earned All-America honors in 1941. He was also an All-SEC pick that same year. Huber actually came to UK on a tennis scholarship after winning state titles at St. Xavier as a sophomore and as a senior. (The finals were rained out his junior

year.) As a prep hoopster, he earned All-State honors after leading St. X to the Sweet 16.

At UK, Huber, although not a big scorer, did have some nice outings. He hit for double figures on twelve occasions, with a career-best 17-point performance against Clemson during his junior campaign.

45. False. Even though Jim Master was a superb free throw shooter—he once hit 40 straight—it is Travis Ford who owns the record. He sank 50 consecutive freebies in a streak that carried over from 1992–93 to 1993–94. For his career, Ford's free throw percentage was 88.2, third best in UK history after Jodie Meeks and Kyle Macy, both of whom hit 89 percent of their free throws. Master's 84.9 percent holds down fourth place.

2

STARTER LEVEL

(Answers begin on Page 65)

1. What former Wildcat had three brothers who played on UK's football squad?

2. Whose acrobatic last-second tip-in lifted the Wildcats past Arizona in the 1993 Maui Classic championship game?

3. Who is the ex-Wildcat who coached Owensboro High School to state titles in 1972 and 1980?

4. Name the Wildcat who came within two points of earning entry into the elite 1,000-point club.

5. <u>MATCH THESE WILDCATS WITH THEIR NICKNAME</u>

<u>Player</u>	<u>Nickname</u>
1. Earl Adkins	a. Jorts
2. Dwight Anderson	b. Golden Greek
3. Kenton Campbell	c. Blade
4. John DeMoisey	d. Worm
5. Leroy Edwards	e. Skippy
6. Randy Embry	f. Brother
7. Allen Feldhaus	g. Herky
8. Jack Givens	h. Blur
9. Phil Grawemeyer	i. Big
10. Joe Hagan	j. Mr. Wildcat
11. Josh Harrellson	k. Aggie

12. Bill Keightley	l. Odie
13. Ronnie Lyons	m. Cowboy
14. Lawrence McGinnis	n. Little
15. Louis McGinnis	o. Sky
16. Adolph Rupp Jr.	p. Horse
17. Forest Sale	q. Frenchy
18. Adrian Smith	r. Goose
19. Henry Thomas	s. Chick
20. Lou Tsioropoulos	t. Cookie
21. Kenny Walker	u. Red
22. Lucian Whitaker	v. Dutch

6. Who was the first Wildcat player to grace the cover of *Sports Illustrated* magazine?

7. Who was the UK broadcaster who later became the play-by-play announcer for the Cincinnati Reds?

8. What ex-Cat spent nearly two years in a German POW camp during World War II?

9. Who is the only Wildcat to win championships at the high school, college, and pro levels?

10. Name the first UK player to have his jersey retired.

11. Who is the highest-scoring father-son duo who played for UK?

12. What two Wildcats share the record for pulling down the most rebounds in a game?

13. Which UK player was the leading scorer for the gold medal–winning US team in the 1948 Olympic Games in London?

14. What Wildcat nailed a last-second jumper to beat Duke in the championship game of the 1963 Sugar Bowl Tournament?

15. Name the Wildcat who hit all 11 of his shots and scored 32 points in an NCAA tourney win over Western Kentucky University.

16. Which two Wildcats share the single-game record for most points scored by a freshman?

17. The Wildcats scored a school-record 143 points during a 1956 game. Who was the opponent?

18. What Wildcat holds the record for most blocked shots in a game?

19. Name the player who owns the record for having played in the most games in a UK uniform.

20. Who scored 23 points and led the Wildcats back from a 31-point second-half deficit in a win at LSU?

21. What Wildcat has the highest single-season field goal percentage?

22. The day after a bitter NCAA tourney loss, Joe B. Hall was asked how he slept that night. "I slept like a baby; I was up every two hours, crying." What team handed UK that loss?

23. Name the UK player who shut down Notre Dame All-American Tom Hawkins during the 1958–59 campaign.

24. What Wildcat was the leading scorer on Adolph Rupp's last team and Joe B. Hall's first team?

25. Name the three visiting teams that participated in the first UKIT.

26. What two former Wildcats were named to the All-NBA first team in 1951?

27. Bill Keightley worked at what job during his early years as the team's equipment manager?

28. Who was UK's first opponent at Memorial Coliseum?

29. Cawood Ledford said this player "picked up the banner and went to war." Who was that player?

30. What sportswriter left Hazard, moved to Lexington in 1975, and started a new publication that covered UK sports?

31. Seventeen former UK players were honored as Kentucky high school Mr. Basketball. Can you name five?

32. In what year did the first of two UK teams fashion an undefeated record?

33. What player's dismissal from the team earned Adolph Rupp a public rebuke from UK's president?

34. Who was the gum-chewing guard whose two free throws gave UK its first NIT title in 1946?

35. What opponent gave arguably the best one-man performance ever against the Wildcats?

36. Which team seemed to own UK during Adolph Rupp's early years as head coach?

37. Who was the all-time great player who once beat UK despite playing with a broken nose?

38. In head-to-head matchups, how many times did UCLA coach John Wooden beat Adolph Rupp?

39. Who won the legendary "Battle of the Giants" during the 1950–51 season?

40. Name the only Wildcat player to be voted SEC Tournament MVP twice.

STARTER ANSWERS

1. Jerry Bird. His three younger brothers, Calvin, Billy, and Rodger all played for the football Cats, with Calvin and Rodger being standout performers. The Bird brothers came from Corbin, the small Kentucky community that also gave us the Selvy clan.

   Jerry was a solid basketball player who lettered three years. As a sophomore, he was a sub on the 1953–54 team that had a 25–0 record. He was a starter the next two seasons, averaging 10.7 points per game as a junior and 16.2 as a senior. His career-best effort was a 34-point performance against Dayton and its seven-foot center Bill Uhl.

   Rodger, the youngest of the four brothers, once told me that he can clearly remember when Adolph Rupp visited the Bird house while attempting to recruit Jerry. Rodger said his parents wanted the three younger brothers out of the way, so he, Calvin, and Billy were sent to a bedroom where they hid while watching and listening as their famous guest made his pitch to Jerry.

Calvin and Rodger were terrific football players at UK. Calvin, who set five school records as a halfback/kick returner, was an All-SEC selection, while Rodger, who scored 25 touchdowns and passed for one, was an All-American. Rodger later played pro football for the Oakland Raiders.

Billy also played at UK, but he didn't have the same level of success as his brothers.

The Bird bunch is one of Kentucky's greatest sports families.

2. Jeff Brassow. With the Cats trailing Arizona 92–91 in the Maul Classic final, the always-alert Brassow somehow managed to tip in a missed shot just ahead of the final horn to give his club the victory.

Brassow was a freshman on Rick Pitino's first UK team, one of the "seven men of iron" who helped that undermanned squad finish with a surprising 14–14 record. As a senior, he tied his career-best effort with 25 points in a win over South Carolina. Later that same season, he tallied 44 points in three SEC Tournament games, including 19 in a 95–76 opening-round win over Mississippi State.

He ended his career with 807 points.

3. Bobby Watson. He ranks as one of the most successful high school coaches in Kentucky prep history, having taken Owensboro High to the Sweet 16 on fourteen occasions, twice coming home with the big trophy.

Watson was also a terrific player as a Wildcat, finishing his career with 1,001 points while playing on some of UK's greatest teams. Because Watson was small (5'10"), there was no shortage of skeptics (including Adolph Rupp) who didn't think he could succeed at UK. Rupp was forever trying to keep him out of the starting lineup, but he couldn't. Watson was simply too good to sit on the bench.

Watson, a superb ball handler and an excellent outside scoring threat, came to UK from Owensboro, where he had been a teammate of the younger Cliff Hagan. Those two, along with Frank Ramsey and Bill Spivey, were at the heart of two genuinely great Wildcat teams.

The 1950–51 club finished with a 32–2 record and won the NCAA Tournament. The next season, despite not having Spivey available, the Cats went 29–3. Overall, during Watson's three years as a starter, UK had a record of 86–10.

He averaged 10.4 on the championship team and 13.2 as a senior. His highest-scoring game was a 27-point effort in a win over Tulane.

4. Jared Prickett. This big, rugged rebounder and defender ended his career with 998 points while playing in 143 games. He also speared 777 rebounds, recorded nine double-doubles, and shot 51.3 percent from the field during his career. He was not a great talent but he sure was a dependable performer.

He came to UK as part of a dynamic recruiting class that included Tony Delk, Rodrick Rhodes, and Walter McCarty. He started 12 games as a freshman, hitting for a season-best 22 points against Florida in the NCAA Tournament.

As a sophomore, he registered a double-double (17-15) against UMass, then grabbed 20 rebounds against Arkansas.

After receiving a medical redshirt following an injury during his senior year, he came back as a fifth-year senior to average 7.9 points and 5.9 rebounds.

Prickett spent several successful years playing overseas.

5. Here are the answers to Match These Wildcats With Their Nickname:

1. f, Earl "Brother" Adkins

2. h, Dwight "Blur" Anderson

3. v, Kenton "Dutch" Campbell

4. q, John "Frenchy" DeMoisey

5. m, Leroy "Cowboy" Edwards

6. s, Randy "Chick" Embry

7. p, Allen "Horse" Feldhaus

8. r, Jack "Goose" Givens

9. t, Phil "Cookie" Grawemeyer

10. u, Joe "Red" Hagan

11. a, Josh "Jorts" Harrellson

12. j, Bill "Mr. Wildcat" Keightley

13. d, Ronnie "Worm" Lyons

14. i, Lawrence "Big" McGinnis

15. n, Louis "Little" McGinnis

16. g, Adolph F. "Herky" Rupp Jr.

17. k, Forest "Aggie" Sale

18. l, Adrian "Odie" Smith

19. c, Henry "Blade" Thomas

20. b, Lou "Golden Greek" Tsioropoulos

21. o, Kenny "Sky" Walker

22. e, Lucian "Skippy" Whitaker

Over the years, several other Wildcats also had worthy nicknames. Two were so easy I didn't even bother to include them: Wallace "Wah Wah" Jones and Charles "Cotton" Nash.

A few others include: Homer "Tub" Thompson, Carl "Hoot" Combs, Lovell "Cowboy" Underwood, Fred "Cab" Curtis, Marvin "Big Train" Akers, Layton "Mickey" Rouse, Mulford "Muff" Davis, C. M. "Fig" Newton, Jay "White Lightning" Shidler, John "Red" Pelphrey, Melvin "Dinner Bell Mel" Turpin, and Jim "Pencil" Master.

Ex-Cat Henry Thomas swears there are many more, most of which, in order to protect the guilty, have to be kept locked safely in the vault.

6. Ralph Beard. The fiery guard, still considered by many as UK's greatest-ever backcourt player, graced the cover of the original *Sports Illustrated* in February 1949. It's a photo of Beard in his white UK uniform, dribbling low, mouth open as if he's yelling at an opponent to get out of his way.

The cost of that issue: a full twenty-five cents. *Sports Illustrated* was originally published by Dell, but that version failed to succeed with the public. Later, Dell sold the rights to Time-Life, which began putting out the magazine as it is seen today. Milwaukee Braves slugger Eddie Mathews was the first player on the cover of that version of the magazine, but that was a full five years after Beard's appearance.

In all, nearly two dozen UK players or coaches have been featured on the *Sports Illustrated* cover.

In 1949, Beard was also featured on the cover of *Clair Bee's Basketball Annual* magazine.

7. Claude Sullivan. Back in the glory days, long before television took over, the Memorial Coliseum floor was ringed by broadcasting crews, and Sullivan was considered the best of them all. A quick glance around the court and you would see Sullivan, Cawood Ledford, J. B. Faulconer, and Phil Sutterfield all describing the action for the listening public. Later, Jim Host, Earl Boardman, and Wah Wah Jones also did some broadcasting of UK games.

Sullivan called his first UK game in 1945, and in 1951 he organized the Standard Oil Sports Network. In 1964, he joined the Cincinnati Reds broadcast team, playing second fiddle to the veteran Waite Hoyt. When Hoyt retired, Sullivan became the No. 1 guy.

Sullivan and Cawood Ledford were such good announcers, and both had remarkably loyal followings, that UK athletics director Bernie Shively held off doing what other SEC schools had begun to do in the 1960s—go to an exclusivity situation on its radio broadcasts and form a single UK radio network.

Shively wouldn't go that route because he wasn't willing to give up Claude or Cawood. There was some talk that they would share the game-day play-by-play duties—each man doing a half—but that notion never materialized. That's because it was around this time that Sullivan became seriously ill. Tragically, the man who made his living with his voice died of throat cancer in 1967 at the age of forty-two.

Sullivan was named Kentucky's Outstanding Sportscaster eight times.

8.   Cliff Barker. The oldest member of the Fabulous Five was serving as an engineer and gunner on a B-17 bomber when it was shot down during World War II, landing him in a German POW camp for almost two years. General George Patton's Third Army freed Barker from the Germans.

It was in the camp, while playing around with a volleyball that had been provided to the prisoners by the Red Cross, that he perfected his magical ball-handling skills.

A former sportswriter once claimed that "Barker could do everything with a basketball except make it talk."

He actually came to UK in the late 1930s, played part of his freshman year, dropped out of school, got married, and joined the Air Force. After the war ended he returned to UK and played on two NCAA championship teams and a gold medal–winning Olympic team.

The 1947–48 team—the Fabulous Five— didn't become that celebrated unit until Barker was inserted into the lineup. Like teammate Kenny Rollins, Barker was an unselfish player who was more than happy to see Alex Groza, Ralph Beard, Wah Wah Jones, Joe Holland, or Jim Line score points and get the big headlines. Barker was far too mature to worry about the petty stuff.

I once asked Beard if the players were scared of Adolph Rupp, who one local scribe called "der fuehrer of basketball doings at the University of Kentucky."

"Well, I was darn scared of him, that's for sure," Ralph answered. "But keep in mind that I was seventeen, eighteen years old when I came to UK. A guy like Barker wasn't in the least bit scared or intimidated. Heck, he'd spent nearly two years in a German prison camp. What could

Coach Rupp possibly say that would scare him? Nothing, that's what."

Barker was twenty-seven years old during his final season as a Wildcat. After leaving UK, he joined with Groza, Beard, Jones, Joe Holland, and Jack Parkinson to form the Indianapolis Olympians in the NBA.

9. Cliff Hagan. The magnificent hook shot artist led Owensboro High School to the Kentucky state title in 1949, UK to the NCAA crown in 1951, and the St. Louis Hawks to the NBA championship in 1958. In addition to that, he led the Wildcats to a 25–0 record during the 1953–54 season.

That powerful team did not participate in the NCAA Tournament because Hagan, Frank Ramsey, and Lou Tsioropoulos were not eligible due to the fact that they were graduate students. They had remained in school during 1952–53 when the team was on probation and not allowed to play. In short, as Hagan once said, "We were punished for doing the right thing."

La Salle, a team UK beat 73–60 in the UKIT finals, won the NCAA title that season.

Cawood Ledford, like Adolph Rupp, would never pick his all-time starting five, but he did tell me once that "anyone who names an all-time starting five that fails to include Cliff Hagan doesn't have a clue what he's talking about."

Only a dummy would argue with Cawood.

10. Layton "Mickey" Rouse. If you are fans of a good mystery, well, here you'll find one that Sherlock Holmes would have a difficult time solving.

Although Rouse was a three-year starter in the backcourt (1938–40), why he was the first UK player to have his jersey retired is a question only Adolph Rupp could answer. His scoring averages were 4.4, 5.4, and 8.3, and his single-game career high was 14 points, which he hit on two occasions. He did earn All-SEC and All-SEC tourney recognition during his senior year.

In the spring of 1940, at the postseason banquet, Rupp presented Rouse with his game jersey (No. 10), which became the first to be retired.

There were many far superior players who preceded Rouse, including All-Americans and Helms Foundation National Players of the Year like Aggie Sale (who Rupp once said may have been the best player he ever coached) and Cowboy Edwards, but it was the low-scoring Rouse who was the first to be immortalized. And the mystery lingers.

11. Allen and Deron Feldhaus. Thanks to Deron's 1,231 points, this honor goes to the "Horse" and his son. Allen was a strong rebounder, defender, and all-around tough cookie, but he was never a big scorer. For his career, Allen scored 299 points, giving the two Feldhaus guys a total of 1,530 points.

The closest competitors to the Feldhaus duo are Terry and Cameron Mills, both of whom were excellent shooters. Terry's best season was in 1969–70 when he averaged 9.1 points per game. Terry tallied 424 points during his days as a Wildcat.

Cameron, a former walk-on who earned a full scholarship, left UK after his senior season having made good on 47.4 percent of his shots from three-point range. As a junior in 1996–97, he made good on 53.2 percent of his treys.

Cameron played a big role in UK's 1998 NCAA championship run, knocking down a critical three-pointer against Duke and then coming back to score eight points in the title-game win over Utah.

Combining Cameron's UK total of 365 points with his father's adds up to 789 points.

Other UK father/son duos include Joe Holland and his son Joey, and Jim and Preston LeMaster. Joe Holland scored 504 points and Joey had 14, while Jim LeMaster finished with 186 points and Preston with 30.

12. Bill Spivey and Bob Burrow. Both of these outstanding centers pulled down 34 rebounds in a single game. Spivey did it against Xavier in 1951, while Burrow did it against Temple in 1955.

Raking in missed shots was the norm for these two players; both knew how to beat opponents to the errant shot. Spivey averaged

17.2 rebounds in 1950–51, pulling down 567 rebounds, a single-season record that still stands today. He also scored 1,213 points in his two seasons as a Wildcat.

Burrow, who also only played two seasons, averaged 17.7 rebounds per game in 1954–55, which remains a school record. Burrow's career average of 16.1 rebounds ranks as the all-time best.

The only other Wildcat to snare 30 rebounds in a game is Cotton Nash, who did it twice, the first time coming against Temple in 1961 and the second time against Ole Miss in 1964.

Here's a statistic that will boggle your mind: In the game against Ole Miss—a 102–59 UK win—the Wildcats pulled down an incredible 108 rebounds. Along with Nash's 30, Ted Deeken had 17, Larry Conley and Terry Mobley had 12 apiece, and Tommy Kron had 11.

To have that many rebounds translates into some horrendous shooting by Ole Miss. It also means they fired up so many shots their arms probably had to be iced down after the game ended. If you need proof that the game of basketball has changed dramatically over the years, consider this: During the 1963–64 season, UK and its opponents combined to average 145.7 shots per game. In 2015–16, that figure had dropped to 117.5 shots per game.

And you wonder why scoring nowadays is so much lower than it once was.

13. Alex Groza. During the 1948 Olympic squad's run to the gold medal, Groza scored a team-best 78 points in those seven encounters. This certainly came as no great shock to Big Blue fans, because by this stage in his career he had become a scoring machine.

The US squad only had one close call during those games in London. That came against Argentina. With three minutes remaining and the score knotted at 55–55, Wildcat Kenny Rollins dropped in a free throw to put the US in front for good. In the end, the US hung on for a 59–57 victory. Groza accounted for 11 points in that win.

After the US romped past Egypt 66–28, Groza had 19 as the US crushed Mexico 71–40. Groza then came back to score 11 points in the 65–21 medal-winning game against France.

Groza averaged 20.5 points per game as a senior in 1948–49, and when he left UK he was the school's all-time leading scorer with 1,744 points. A three-time All-American, he was instrumental in leading UK to back-to-back NCAA titles.

His brother, Lou "The Toe" Groza was an outstanding placekicker for the Cleveland Browns and is a member of the Pro Football Hall of Fame.

14. Terry Mobley. With the undefeated Wildcats on the short end of a 79–77 score with just under two minutes to play, Mobley, who had made

Terry Mobley put the hurt on
Duke in the 1963 Sugar Bowl
Tournament.
*Photo courtesy of University of
Kentucky Athletics.*

only one bucket in the first thirty-eight minutes,
connected on a short jumper to tie the score at
79–79. Moments later, Ted Deeken swatted
away a pass and Tommy Kron came up with
the loose ball, which he then passed ahead to
Mobley.

Mobley wasn't the first or obvious choice to
take the last shot—All-American Cotton Nash

was. But when Mobley saw that Nash was being blanketed by Duke's towering front line, he drove down the left side of the foul lane, pulled up and nailed the game-winning bucket.

That victory improved the Cats' record to 10–0 and vaulted them to No. 1 in the national polls for the first time since 1959. Having reached the top, they promptly lost their next two games, going from first in the nation to last in the SEC. But they quickly got back on track, winning the SEC title with an 11–3 league record. Overall, that club finished with a 21–6 mark.

15. Kenny Walker. It took every ounce of Walker's perfect performance for the Cats to earn that hard-fought 71–64 victory over the Hilltoppers in NCAA tourney action. This would be the first time the two schools clashed since a 1971 tourney game won by WKU 107–83.

Thanks to Walker's great effort, the Cats managed to get past the Hilltoppers. That club, Eddie Sutton's first as UK coach, finished with a 32–4 record before being eliminated by an LSU team the Cats had beaten three times that season.

Walker, a marked man every time he stepped on the court, averaged 22.9 points as a junior and 20.0 as a senior.

The high-jumping Walker left as UK's second all-time leading scorer with 2,080 career points, making him one of only three Wildcats to break the 2,000-point mark. He also had 942 rebounds and blocked 122 shots.

Walker was twice named SEC Player of the Year. The New York Knicks chose him in the first round of the 1986 NBA draft. In 1989, he won the NBA Slam Dunk competition.

16. Terrence Jones and Jamal Murray. Jones's 35-point effort came against Auburn in 2011. Jones actually came off the bench in that game, making good on 11 of 17 field goal attempts, including four beyond the three-point arc.

Putting up big numbers was nothing new for Jones, who scored 1,064 in his two years at UK. He scored 29 against Oklahoma, 27 against Notre Dame, and 25 on two occasions, against Vanderbilt and East Tennessee State.

Jones averaged 15.7 points as a freshman and 12.3 as a sophomore, while recording 17 double-doubles.

Murray's monster effort came against Florida in 2016. In that outing, he nailed 13 of 21 shots, including making good on 8 of 10 from beyond the three-point line. Earlier in the season, the gifted Murray scored 33 against Ohio State and he also had 33 against Vanderbilt three weeks after the Florida game.

Other freshmen who topped the 30-point mark are Doron Lamb (32 vs. Winthrop in 2010), Jamal Mashburn (31 vs. Georgia in 1991), and Brandon Knight (30 vs. West Virginia in 2011).

17. Georgia. Playing at the Louisville Armory, and coming off a humiliating 101–77 loss to Alabama (this was the first opponent to score 100 points

against UK), the Cats vented their frustration by demolishing Georgia 143–66 late in the 1955–56 season. This still stands as the most points scored by a UK team.

In this win, Jerry Bird led the way with 22 points, while Bob Burrow added 21. In all, thirteen different Wildcats scored.

This was a fairly decent UK team, one some thought might do well in NCAA Tournament action. The motivation to excel was certainly present. After all, just being in the tournament was a gift. Alabama won the SEC title with a flawless 14–0 record, but declined to participate in the NCAA Tournament because school officials didn't want to risk having to play against black players. By virtue of their 12–2 second-place finish in the league standings, the Cats were given the bid.

But it didn't take long before it became evident that this Wildcat team probably wasn't going to go very deep into the tournament. In the opener, the Cats trailed Wayne State 38–36 before finally waking up in time to avoid complete embarrassment. Behind 33 points from Burrow, 14 by Gerry Calvert, and 10 each by Bird and Vernon Hatton, the Cats pulled away for an 84–64 victory.

The season came to a crashing halt in the Cats' next outing, an 89–77 loss to Iowa. All-American Carl "Sugar" Cain ripped the Cats for 34 points. Burrow had 31 and Bird 23 in a losing cause.

18. Nerlens Noel. Although the guy couldn't make a bucket if he was more than five feet from the goal, he sure had a knack for swatting away enemy shots. He set the school record with 12 blocked shots against Ole Miss in 2013.

Noel had 106 blocked shots in his one season at UK, an average of 4.4.

Willie Cauley-Stein (twice), Andre Riddick, and Sam Bowie are all tied for second place with nine blocks each.

19. Darius Miller. The Maysville native played in 152 games from 2008–12, breaking the old mark of 151 held by Wayne Turner (1996–99). Kenny Walker owns the record for games played against Southeastern Conference opponents with 72.

Other Wildcats who suited up on many occasions include Jamaal Magloire (145), Saul Smith and Jared Prickett (143), and Anthony Epps (141).

The great Ralph Beard holds the mark for most games started with 136.

20. Walter McCarty. Seldom in UK's long history has there been a more improbable victory than the one dubbed the "Mardi Gras Miracle." And it was truly a miracle. With LSU up by 31 points at the sixteen-minute mark, the fans in the Maravich Assembly Center had already begun to celebrate.

But the celebration turned out to be premature. With reserves McCarty, Chris Harrison, and Jeff Brassow leading the comeback charge, the Cats began to whittle away at the LSU advantage. As things got tighter, the LSU crowd got quieter. No doubt, they were having a hard time believing what was happening right in front of them.

The gap kept closing until McCarty buried a three-pointer that put UK in front 96–95 with 19 seconds remaining. The Cats finished off the historic comeback by sinking three of four free throws while holding LSU scoreless.

McCarty led a balanced scoring attack with 23 points. Others in double digits included Brassow (14), Gimel Martinez (13), Rodrick Rhodes (11), and Travis Ford (10). Tony Delk and Andre Riddick each contributed nine points.

This marked the greatest comeback in UK history.

21. Michael Bradley. Even though he didn't last long at UK he earned a spot in the record books by making good on 65.7 percent of his shots during the 1998–99 season. That year he hit 157 of 239 attempts.

At 6'10", Bradley was mobile, quick and a good shooter. After not contributing much in his rookie season, he came back as a sophomore, started every game and performed with solid consistency. His scoring average that season was 9.8 points per game.

But Bradley had been recruited by Rick Pitino, who gave the Bradley family his assurance that he wasn't leaving UK. Then, before the school year, Pitino left for Boston.

Bradley played two seasons for Tubby Smith, and then surprised everyone by announcing that he was leaving UK after the 1998–99 campaign.

The UK career-best record of 60.2 percent belongs to Marquis Estill (2001–03), who connected on 365 of 606 attempts.

22. Georgetown University. This disappointing 53–40 NCAA tourney semifinal loss is remembered for UK's dismal 3-for-33 shooting in the second half. That computes to a particularly horrid 9.1 percent.

Things had unfolded in a much more positive manner—the Cats hit 50 percent in the first half (10 of 20), and were on top 29–22 at intermission. At this stage it looked like the Cats were on their way to comfortably handling Patrick Ewing and his Hoyas teammates.

But then everything went south. Or north, depending on how far you want to travel before bumping into a glacier. In those final twenty minutes the Cats were colder than a Siberian winter. So cold, in fact, that it took almost ten minutes before Winston Bennett scored the Cats' first second-half bucket.

By then the Hoyas were in complete control, and Hall was on his way to a sleepless night.

23. Billy Ray Lickert. During his sophomore season Lickert gave a monster performance against Notre Dame, scoring 24 points and grabbing 17 rebounds while holding Hawkins to 13 points,

11 below his average. Thanks to Lickert, the Cats won it 71–52.

This was just one of many terrific efforts by the steady Lickert, who was named Kentucky's Mr. Basketball after leading Lexington Lafayette to the Kentucky high school championship in 1957.

As a junior, he also gave a brilliant 29-point effort in UK's 96–93 victory over a powerful Ohio State club that featured Jerry Lucas, John Havlicek, and Larry Siegfried. That performance came after he opened the season by hitting for 23 points against UCLA, 20 against St. Louis, and 27 against Temple. As a senior he had another red-hot stretch, racking up 106 points in four games.

Lickert, a three-time All-SEC pick who scored 1,076 career points, is one of the most complete players to ever wear the UK blue and white.

24. Jim Andrews. The big 6'11" center from Lima, Ohio, averaged 21.5 points per game as a junior on Adolph Rupp's final team in 1971–72. The next season, with Joe B. Hall at the helm, Andrews scored at a 20.1 clip.

Because UK has had so many great pivot players—Groza, Spivey, Issel, Robey, Bowie, Cousins, Davis, and Towns, just to name a few— Andrews often gets lost in the shuffle. That's a big mistake; he was a terrific player and should be recognized as such.

He had some really big-time scoring games—37 versus Northwestern, 34 versus Mississippi State and Vanderbilt, 33 versus Oregon, and 32 against Michigan State and Georgia.

He was also a monster on the boards, once grabbing 21 rebounds against Mississippi State.

For his career, Andrews scored 1,320 points while hitting 56.3 percent of his field goal attempts.

25. La Salle, Duke, and UCLA. Talk about a high-profile trio, here it is. The inaugural event was played on December 21–22 in 1953. Although no one knew it at the time, the UKIT turned out to be this UK team's NCAA Tournament. The UKIT also proved to be a financial windfall for the three visiting teams, each of which netted approximately $10,000, making this the most lucrative holiday classic in the country.

La Salle, led by high-scoring All-American Tom Gola, topped John Wooden's Bruins in the tourney opener. In their first-round game, the Cats had no trouble with Duke, winning handily 85–69.

In the championship game, with Cliff Hagan outscoring Gola 28–16, the Cats rolled to a convincing 73–60 victory. The Cats were in control from the start in this battle, grabbing a 16–13 lead after one quarter, then steadily adding to their margin as the game wore on.

Along with Hagan, Lou Tsioropoulos and Phil Grawemeyer also played well, scoring 18 and 13 points, respectively.

Remember, this was the year the Cats went undefeated but didn't participate in the NCAA festivities. Three months after the UKIT, with the Wildcat players forced to watch from a distance, La Salle won the NCAA championship.

26. Ralph Beard and Alex Groza. These two, along with Fabulous Five teammates Wah Wah Jones, Cliff Barker, and Joe Holland, were part owners of the NBA's Indianapolis Olympians franchise they formed. Another ex-Cat, Jack Parkinson, also played on the squad.

The Olympians were successful on the court and at the box office. They were all well on their way to becoming financially successful athletes. And in only their second year as pros, Beard and Groza made the All-NBA first-team.

Sadly, this was their final hurrah. Because they were implicated in the point-shaving scandal of the late 1940s, they were banned for life from playing in the NBA, ending the careers of two players who undoubtedly would have been in the Basketball Hall of Fame.

The Olympians, minus Groza and Beard, limped on for a year or so, with Jones doing all he could the keep things going, but in the end he couldn't do it by himself and the franchise folded.

27. Mail carrier. The venerable "Mr. Wildcat" worked for the United States Post Office for many years before retiring to become UK's full-time equipment manager. Well, he was far more than that. He was also a close friend and father confessor to several generations of Wildcat players.

In those early years, Keightley would work a full shift and then head to Memorial Coliseum to fulfill his duties as equipment manager. Oftentimes, after working, he would accompany the team on road games.

Even as he got older, he remained a man with unlimited energy and stamina. It was not unusual for him to be the first guy at work. And the equipment room, a place where players came to vent their frustrations and friends dropped by to chat, was Mr. Wildcat's own little sanctuary.

After C. M. Newton retired as AD, Keightley was the last link to the days of Adolph Rupp.

It was Joe B. Hall who first dubbed Keightley as "Mr. Wildcat."

28. West Texas State. The first game played in the new gym took place on December 1, 1950, and with a starting quintet of Bill Spivey, Shelby Linville, Walt Hirsch, Bobby Watson, and Frank Ramsey, the Wildcats routed the visitors 73–43.

When it was first announced that UK was going to spend around four million dollars to build a new basketball arena, the critics began chirping like a battalion of crickets. In their eyes it was simply a waste of money that could better be spent elsewhere.

Plus, a gym capable of holding 11,500 could never be filled. Those skeptics simply didn't think basketball was popular enough to consistently fill a building with such a large capacity. Many of them called it a "white elephant."

The first team to play in the new gym was a strong one, and once Cliff Hagan became eligible at mid-semester, it became even stronger. The Cats proved their strength by beating Kansas State 68–58 to capture the NCAA title, giving UK its third championship in the past four years.

As for the critics, well, history proved them wrong. Memorial Coliseum, built to honor the Kentuckians who died in World War II (and later the Korean conflict and Vietnam War), was consistently filled to capacity. And basketball turned out to be so popular that a few decades later Memorial Coliseum became too small, eventually giving way to Rupp Arena, which has almost twice the seating capacity of its predecessor.

29. Mike Pratt. Few Wildcats have been tougher than this guy. During his fabulous three-year career he turned in some of the most-memorable performances ever given by a UK player, and none was greater or more memorable than the one against a formidable Notre Dame club led by All-American Austin Carr.

In what ended up being a ferocious struggle, the Cats, fueled by Pratt's 42 points, edged the

Irish 102–100 at Louisville's Freedom Hall. At some point during the game, Cawood made his "gone to war" statement about Pratt. It was a phrase that became part of the UK lexicon, a way to describe outstanding individual efforts.

For his career, Pratt finished with 1,359 points. He then went on to play professionally, and is currently a member of the UK broadcast team.

30. Oscar Combs. The idea came to him after speaking with three fans at a UK road game who said they had never seen the Wildcats play in person until that day. They had become Big Blue fans by listening to Cawood Ledford call the games on radio.

In 1975, Combs came to Lexington with the dream of starting a publication that would cover UK basketball and football. If those faraway fans couldn't see their heroes in person, Combs would at least make it possible for them to know what was going on with their beloved Wildcats.

Joe B. Hall was an early supporter of the idea, but football coach Fran Curci was less enthusiastic. Cliff Hagan, UK's athletics director, initially straddled the fence, but later gave it his blessing.

Combs named his weekly publication *The Cats' Pause*, and it was the first of its kind in college sports. During its heyday *The Cats' Pause* had a circulation of 22,000.

31. Here are the 17 former Wildcats who were named Mr. Basketball: Billy Ray Lickert (1957), Pat Doyle (1959), Randy Embry (1961), Mike Casey (1966), Jimmy Dan Conner (1971), Jack Givens (1974), Dirk Minniefield (1979), Todd May (1982), Winston Bennett (1983), Rex Chapman (1986), John Pelphrey (1987), Richie Farmer (1988), Josh Carrier (2001), Brandon Stockton (2002), Darius Miller (2008), Jon Hood (2009), and Dominique Hawkins (2013). How many did you name?

32. The 1911–12 club finished with a flawless 9–0 record and was crowned Southern Champions after edging Georgetown 19–18 in the season's final game.

This was an unusually high-scoring team for the time, averaging 31.2 points per game. The best effort was a 52-point performance against Central University.

The leading scorer that season was Binkley Barnett with a 7.1 average. Other team members included D. W. Hart, W. C. Harrison, Jake Gaiser, R. C. Preston, H. L. Farmer, and William Tuttle.

The coach of that perfect team was E. R. Sweetland.

33. Bobby Tallent. After having an excellent sophomore season as backup guard on the 1965–66 Rupp's Runts team, Tallent, who played for Maytown High School, moved into the starting lineup as a junior in 1966–67.

With starters Louie Dampier, Pat Riley, and Thad Jaracz returning from the previous year, expectations for this team were sky-high. But it turned out to be a miserable year, primarily because Riley was hobbled by a nagging injury that kept him from consistently performing at his usual high standards. As a result, this team could do no better than a 13–13 record. Those 13 setbacks and the .500 won-loss mark were by far the worst ever for Adolph Rupp.

Despite it all, Tallent, a marvelous outside shooter, generally acquitted himself well. He scored 20 against both Northwestern and Florida, 25 against Kansas State, 28 against Notre Dame, and 26 in a loss to Florida.

Perhaps inevitably, the strain of such a miserable and disappointing season was bound to manifest in some negative ways. And it did—a clash between Rupp and Tallent.

Hard feelings between the two had been growing since Rupp publicly criticized Tallent for poor ball handling and a lack of good leadership skills. Their feud finally reached the boiling point during a game at Tennessee, when, after Tallent was yanked from the game following a mistake, the two men exchanged harsh words.

The next Monday, when Tallent reported for practice, he discovered that his locker was empty and he was not to be issued any gear. Most UK fans were in agreement that Rupp was being too hard on his junior guard. So did UK president Dr. John Oswald, who summoned Rupp to his office and made it clear that he was not pleased with the way Tallent had been treated. In particular, Oswald expressed his displeasure at Rupp's "public censure" of Tallent.

That made no difference, however. Rupp wasn't about to change his mind, and Bobby Tallent never played in another UK game. He later transferred to George Washington University, where he had an outstanding career.

34. Ralph Beard. Back in those days the National Invitation Tournament (NIT) was considered a far more challenging and prestigious event than the still-young NCAA tourney. Winning the NIT was a big deal.

At the time, participating in the NCAA tourney was, in Beard's words, like "playing in an YMCA tournament."

Beard and Wah Wah Jones were freshmen starters on a unit that also featured Jack Tingle, Wilbur Schu, and Jack Parkinson. The Cats won their first two tourney games, beating Arizona 77–53 and West Virginia 59–51. That earned them a spot in the championship game against Rhode Island.

It was a fierce battle, with twelve ties and no more than four points separating the two combatants during the final seventeen minutes. The Cats, an eight-point favorite, were trailing 45–44 with less than two minutes left when Dutch Campbell made good on one of two free throws to knot the count at 45–45.

The 1946 NIT championship team. Kneeling (l-r): manager Humzey Yessin, Muff Davis, Buddy Parker, Ralph Beard, Jack Parkinson, and Bill Sturgill. Standing (l-r): trainer Frank Mann, Elmer Gilb, Jack Tingle, Dutch Campbell, Adolph Rupp, Wah Wah Jones, Wilbur Schu, and Joe Holland.
Photo courtesy of University of Kentucky Athletics.

Following a Rhode Island miss, the Cats rebounded and got the ball to Beard, who was immediately fouled. With 40 seconds left to play, and with 18,000 charged-up Madison Square Garden fans making their presence felt, the gum-chewing nineteen-year-old Beard stepped to the line and calmly sank the game-deciding point.

Beard led all scorers with 13 points, while his classmate Jones added 10.

This UK club finished with a 28–2 record.

35. Navy's David Robinson. The list of great players who have left their mark on UK is one that includes the likes of Jerry West, Jerry Lucas, Billy Cunningham, Jeff Mullins, Jim McDaniels, Charles Barkley, and Shaquille O'Neal, just to rattle off a few.

And of course there is LSU's Pistol Pete Maravich, who scored those 312 points in six outings against the Wildcats.

However, none of those guys, great as they were, ever did so much destruction to a UK team as Robinson did during a 1987 game in Rupp Arena. All Robinson did was score 45 points, grab 14 rebounds, block 10 shots, and throw down eight dunks.

In the end, though, Robinson was a one-man show. The final: UK 80, Navy 69.

36. Notre Dame. While Rupp's early teams were usually savaging opponents on a regular basis, Notre Dame was the one club that seemed to have UK's number. The first seven times a Rupp-coached team faced the Irish, the Cats walked away losers. And some of those games weren't close. Notre Dame had three wins by double digits (21 points, 13, and 10).

That all changed on the night of January 23, 1943, at Louisville's Jefferson County Armory. Led by Marvin "Big Train" Akers, the Cats erased a 10-point second-half deficit and went on to beat the unbeaten Irish 60–55. With the score tied at 52–52, Mel Brewer scored in the pivot to ignite a 6–0 run that put the Cats in front for good.

Akers paced the Cats with 17 points, while Milt Ticco added 16 and Mulford "Muff" Davis had a dozen.

Following the game, a jubilant Akers said, "It was a great game for Adolph Rupp. He is now thoroughly convinced that all things come to those who wait."

37. Jerry West. Adolph Rupp always counted the West Virginia standout among the two or three greatest opponents UK ever had to deal with. And for good reason. Jerry West is quite simply one of the greatest basketball players to ever put on a uniform.

Three times he led West Virginia into the UKIT, and twice his Mountaineers came away with the championship hardware. As a sophomore, the guy known as "Zeke from Cabin Creek" scored 15 as West Virginia upended UK 77–70 in the opener. Keep in mind that this was the UK team—the Fiddlin' Five—that would go on to capture the national title.

The next two years UK and West Virginia met in the championship game. In the 1958 UKIT final, the Cats clipped West Virginia 97–91 despite 36 points from West. Sid Cohen was the big gun for UK, which played without Billy Ray Lickert, out with a stomach virus. Cohen finished with 23 points. Bobby Slusher had 19, Don Mills 17, and Johnny Cox 16 for the winners.

It was in West Virginia's third appearance in the UKIT that West, his nose broken, led his team to the title for the second time, racking up 33 points in a 79–70 victory. Lickert's early defense held West in check and enabled UK to stay close for much of the first half. But when Lickert was tagged with his fourth foul prior to intermission, West took over.

Many years later, when recalling the difficult task of guarding West, Lickert said, "I think the guy scored six points during the National Anthem."

38. Zero, that's how many. These two coaching titans only met three times and UK won all three games.

The first meeting took place during the 1951–52 season, and the Cats, behind 34 points from Cliff Hagan, ripped Wooden's squad 84–53. That would be the only easy win in this series of battles between the two most successful coaches of all time. The next two games were decided by a grand total of three points.

During the 1959–60 campaign, the Cats, riding a 23-point performance from Billy Ray Lickert, claimed a hard-earned 68–66 victory in Los Angeles. One season later, Roger Newman's 26-point, 18-rebound effort was enough to lift the Cats to a 77–76 win at Memorial Coliseum. Larry Pursiful also had a big night, finishing with 21 points for UK.

Rupp and Wooden won fourteen NCAA championships between them.

39. Bill Spivey. This was billed as a "Battle of the Giants" because Spivey, at 7'0", and 6'9" Kansas center Clyde Lovellette were regarded as the top two big men in the college ranks at the time. Because of those two, and also because Adolph Rupp would be coaching against his college coach, Phog Allen, this game generated intense interest.

With 13,000 excited fans crammed into brand-new Memorial Coliseum, the two teams— and the two centers—went at it. And neither outcome was close. It was a total mismatch from a team standpoint and in the individual duel between Spivey and Lovellette.

The Cats led 28–12 at intermission, then went on to register a 68–39 win. In that opening half, Spivey and Frank Ramsey accounted for 22 of those 28 points.

As for the Spivey-Lovellette showdown, Spivey easily dominated his opposing center, outscoring Lovellette 22–10. And it could have been worse. After Lovellette committed his fifth and final foul, Rupp removed Spivey from the game for good. There was still 13:33 left to play.

Spivey would go on to become one of the most unjustly treated athletes in sports history. He was forced to sit out his senior season at UK, and then was permanently banned from playing in the NBA despite never having been found guilty of either being involved in the point-shaving scandal or a later perjury charge. As a result, he ended up playing in exhibition games against the Harlem Globetrotters.

He later sued the NBA and won a big judgment, but by then it was too late. The damage had already been done.

Here is something you can take to the bank. Had Spivey played his senior year, that 1951–52 team would have been UK's greatest ever. Hands down the best. That team went 29–3 without Spivey, who was arguably the best big man in the game, both at the college and NBA levels. If he had been on that team, UK would have captured another NCAA title.

When Spivey came to UK from Warner Robins, Georgia, he was as skinny as he was tall. Rupp realized that if Spivey was going to be a successful basketball player, he needed to put on some weight. This meant drinking plenty of milk shakes and taking two trays of food each time he went through the line in the school cafeteria.

Since Rupp was involved with the Olympics that summer, he gave assistant coach Harry Lancaster the double assignment of working with Spivey on his basketball skills and with helping him gain the much-needed weight. Over the summer, Lancaster sent a series of telegrams to Rupp, and in one, Lancaster boasted that Spivey had gained twelve pounds.

Bill Spivey was one of the most unjustly treated athletes in sports history.

Photo courtesy of University of Kentucky Athletics.

"I know he can eat," Rupp replied, "but can he play basketball?"

Yes, he could.

40. Travis Ford. This Madisonville native transferred to UK after playing his freshman season at the University of Missouri. That turned out to be a good deal for the Wildcats, because Ford was one of those rare backcourt aces who combined a deadly shooting touch with a point guard mentality.

His initial season at UK was plagued with injuries that slowed him down. However, once he got healthy he became one of UK's most-productive guards. He scored at a 13.6 clip as a junior and 11.3 in his final season.

Ford earned the first of those two SEC Tournament MVP awards after scoring 26 points against Arkansas and 18 against LSU. In UK's three wins he canned 14 of 22 three-pointers.

One year later, Ford picked up his second consecutive MVP trophy after helping the Cats beat Mississippi State, Arkansas, and Florida to win their third straight SEC tourney title.

Ford connected on 44.5 percent of his three-point attempts during his UK career.

3

ALL-AMERICAN LEVEL

(Answers begin on Page 108)

1. Adolph Rupp came to UK after coaching high school basketball and wrestling in what state?

2. What player was UK's youngest All-American?

3. Who was the fiery coach who complained prior to an NCAA tourney game because the ball being used had Adolph Rupp's name on it?

4. What Wildcat led a rebellion and left the team during the 1954–55 season?

5. **MATCH THESE WILDCATS WITH THEIR JERSEY NUMBER**

Player	Number
1. Phil Argento	a. 77
2. Dale Barnstable	b. 23
3. Keith Bogans	c. 42
4. Sam Bowie	d. 22
5. Bob Brannum	e. 33
6. John Brewer	f. 54
7. Bob Burrow	g. 55
8. Ralph Carlisle	h. 41
9. Johnny Cox	i. 6
10. Joe Crawford	j. 10
11. Gerald Fitch	k. 18
12. Phil Grawemeyer	l. 20
13. Cliff Hagan	m. 31

14. Roger Harden   n. 38

15. Thad Jaracz   o. 32

16. Wah Wah Jones p. 34

17. Cameron Mills   q. 44

18. Don Mills   r. 80

19. Randolph Morris s. 4

20. Roger Newman   t. 50

21. Tom Parker   u. 21

22. Scott Padgett   v. 12

23. Mark Pope   w. 24

24. Patrick Sparks   x. 27

25. Bill Spivey   y. 13

26. Bobby Watson   z. 14

6. Thomas Payne was the first black player at UK. Who was the second?

7. Name the ex-Cat whose son was a standout receiver at the University of Florida and for the Cincinnati Bengals, and is currently a well-respected NFL broadcaster.

8. Name five former Wildcats who also led their teams to the Kentucky high school championship.

9. What ex-Wildcat coached Lexington Lafayette to three high school championships?

10. What two UK players were credited with combining to hold Bob Cousy to five points?

11. Which UK team holds the record for having the greatest margin of victory?

12. Who are the only three Wildcats to score 40 or more points in an NCAA Tournament game?

13. What former Wildcat player was the first to coach against—and beat—UK?

14. Name the two big men who came to UK, attended school, but never suited up.

15. Whose miraculous last-second three-point play against Maryland tied the game, which UK won in overtime?

16. Who was UK's president during the NCAA probe in the late 1980s?

17. Prior to UK-Duke in 1992, what game was billed as "the greatest of all-time"?

18. Who is universally recognized as the "father of UK sports history"?

19. What UK president held firm and refused to make an exception that would have allowed Adolph Rupp to keep coaching after reaching the mandatory retirement age?

20. Name the five non-players who have a banner hanging at Rupp Arena.

These next five questions are multiple choice. Be careful and think before answering.

21. Who coached the Wildcats immediately prior to Adolph Rupp taking charge?
(a) W. W. H. Mustaine (b) George Buchheit (c) John Mauer (d) E. R. Sweetland

22. Who was the first junior college player to sign with UK?
(a) Adrian Smith (b) Bob Burrow (c) Sid Cohen (d) Bennie Coffman

23. Name the ex-Wildcat who was also a Methodist minister.
(a) Kenny Rollins (b) Ed Beck (c) Larry Pursiful (d) Cameron Mills

24. Which Wildcat hit the most free throws during an NCAA tourney game?
(a) Cliff Hagan (b) Roger Newman (c) Cotton Nash (d) Dwight Anderson

25. What Wildcat is credited with hitting the longest shot during a game?
(a) Joe "Red" Hagan (b) Ralph Beard (c) Cliff Barker (d) Linville Puckett

ALL-AMERICAN
ANSWERS

1. Illinois. Adolph Rupp was one of seventy coaches who applied for the job when it came open after the 1929–30 season had concluded. He spent the previous three seasons coaching at Freeport (Illinois) High School, where his teams had a 66–17 record, won two district titles and one sectional title. Additionally, he also coached the wrestling team.

   During his interview, when asked why UK should choose him over one of the other candidates, the never-too-modest Rupp replied, "Because I'm the best damned basketball coach in the nation."

   And it didn't take long before he backed up his bold talk.

   Rupp brought with him a new system, namely an up-tempo, fast-breaking style of play. Not everyone was convinced that this new approach would be successful. The *Kernal*, UK's school paper, went so far as to

The 1933 Helms Foundation National Champs. In the back row, fourth and fifth from the left, are All-Americans Aggie Sale and Frenchy DeMoisey.
Photo courtesy of University of Kentucky Athletics.

claim that, "If Coach Rupp does come through with a winning team he will be hailed as a miracle man."

All Rupp's first team did was finish with a 15–3 record. His first five years at UK were incredibly successful, and would set the bar high for future Wildcat teams to aim for. Those five teams went 86–11, with the 1933 club being named Helms Foundation National Champions.

During that time frame six Wildcats earned All-America honors. They were Carey Spicer, Aggie Sale, Ellis Johnson, Frenchy DeMoisey, Leroy Edwards, and Dave Lawrence.

2. Bob Brannum. Although this raw, brawny guy only played one full season at UK he made it a memorable one, helping that youthful 1943–44 "Wildkittens" squad post a surprising 19–2 record. This was the team that featured only freshmen and sophomores on the roster.

Brannum, a 6'5" native of Winfield, Kansas, let the team in scoring with a 12.1 average. He had several big games, perhaps none bigger than the one against Notre Dame. In that game, he scored 14 points, including a game-deciding three-point play that gave the Cats a 55–54 win.

He was eighteen when he was named an All-American.

Brannum left UK after his freshman season and entered the military. When he returned to UK for the 1946–47 season, the talent pool was so deep that he was no longer a starter. The same thing happened to Jack Parkinson when he came out of the service. Both had been named All-Americans, and now they were second-string players.

Prior to the conference tournament, Adolph Rupp revealed the names of the ten-man traveling squad. Brannum was not among those who would be making the trip. Unhappy with that situation, he transferred to Michigan State, where he would have an outstanding career.

Brannum did have one final measure of personal revenge against Adolph Rupp and the Wildcats. During the 1947–48 season, UK hit the road to face off against Brannum and his Michigan State teammates. And it was a battle.

The Cats, thanks to three Kenny Rollins points inside the final 45 seconds and seven clutch points by Dale Barnstable, managed to escape with a 47–45 win.

This game also meant Brannum would be going up against Alex Groza, the man who replaced him as UK's starting center. In their only head-to-head individual battle, Brannum, who had a game-best 23 points, clearly outplayed Groza, who had 10.

3. Al McGuire. Although McGuire became something of a lovable, slightly eccentric sage during his later years as a broadcaster, during his heyday as Marquette coach he seldom strayed far from his true persona, that of a tough, streetwise New Yorker with an acid tongue and a fiercely competitive nature.

He was also not among those Adolph Rupp sent a Christmas card to every year. In fact, Rupp pretty much detested McGuire, who enjoyed getting his digs in against the Baron. This was never more evident than when UK and Marquette met at Memorial Coliseum during the 1968 Mideast Regional.

McGuire, always happy with playing the role of villain, refused to join the other coaches on Rupp's TV show. And even though the game was being played on UK's home court, McGuire demanded that his team be allowed to dress in the home team's locker room and sit on the home team's bench.

Naturally, none of this pleased Rupp, who, in the end, did get in the last word. When McGuire balked at playing the game with a ball that had Rupp's name on it, Rupp said, "Find a ball with your name on it, Al, and that's the one we'll use." McGuire had no comeback for that one.

In the end, handling the Warriors on the court turned out to be easier than handling McGuire off the court. With Dan Issel scoring 36 points (14 of 18 from the field) and grabbing 13 rebounds, the Cats rolled to a 107–89 win.

4. Linville Puckett. This Clark County native was one of the best high school players in Kentucky history, leading his team to the state championship in 1951. He played in the state tourney four years and was a three-time all-tournament team selection. In all, he scored 210 points in Sweet 16 games, including 47 in a 99–59 win over Somerset in 1952.

As a sophomore at UK, he was a valuable contributor on the 1953–54 club that had a 25–0 record. When the next season rolled around, Puckett was expected to be one of the team's standout performers. And when the season kicked off, he was a starter along with Bob Burrow, Jerry Bird, Phil Grawemeyer, and Billy Evans.

Puckett was a steady, dependable backcourt player, helping that team build a 12–2 record.

But then, prior to taking on Florida, Adolph Rupp announced that Puckett had been dismissed from the team for missing practice.

There are several conflicting stories that detail the first open rebellion against Rupp.

According to Russell Rice, the longtime UK sports information director, when the team returned home following a loss to Georgia Tech, the players, who were in the middle of the semester break, decided, against Rupp's rules, to go home overnight. When Rupp heard about this, he scheduled a practice for the next afternoon. Not wanting to miss practice, the players returned to Lexington, agreeing that if Rupp kicked one of them off the team, they would all quit.

Rupp accused his players of not having winning on their minds, and as a punishment he took away their complimentary tickets for the next home game. Hearing that, Puckett stood up and said that if he didn't get his tickets he wasn't going to play. All of his teammates, with the exception of Billy Evans and Dan Chandler, got up and left the room.

Evans was the team captain, so Rupp ordered him to go tell the players that there would be a practice at 3:15 that afternoon, adding that if any player failed to show up, "Harry [Lancaster] and I will put his stuff in the middle of Euclid Avenue."

When Evans saw Puckett leave the room first he assumed Puckett was leading the uprising. The two players met outside and a fight almost took place before other players intervened, explaining to Evans what had happened. They all went back and spoke with Rupp, who again told them to be on the floor at 3:15. Everyone showed up except Puckett, who announced that he was quitting the team.

When asked about it, Puckett responded by saying that basketball at UK was "a matter of life and death," equating the experience with that of going to war.

5. Here are the answers to Match These Wildcats With Their Jersey Number:
   1. y, Phil Argento (13)
   2. k, Dale Barnstable (18)
   3. j, Keith Bogans (10)
   4. m, Sam Bowie (31)
   5. l, Bob Brannum (20)
   6. r, John Brewer (80)
   7. t, Bob Burrow (50)
   8. z, Ralph Carlisle (14)
   9. w, Johnny Cox (24)
   10. o, Joe Crawford (32)
   11. s, Gerald Fitch (4)
   12. q, Phil Grawemeyer (44)
   13. i, Cliff Hagan (6)
   14. b, Roger Harden (23)
   15. g, Thad Jaracz (55)

16. x, Wah Wah Jones (27)

17. u, Cameron Mills (21)

18. f, Don Mills (54)

19. e, Randolph Morris (33)

20. c, Roger Newman (42)

21. v, Tom Parker (12)

22. p, Scott Padgett (34)

23. h, Mark Pope (41)

24. d, Patrick Sparks (22)

25. a, Bill Spivey (77)

26. n, Bobby Watson (38)

6. Reggie Warford. He came to UK after an outstanding career at Drakesboro High School in Muhlenberg County. Even though he only lettered one year as a Wildcat (1975–76), Warford was an important figure in UK history. With his help, UK managed to bring in such outstanding players as Larry Johnson, Jack Givens, James Lee, and Truman Claytor.

Warford was a starter during his senior season, helping lead that club to the NIT championship. The title game turned out to be a showcase for Warford, who scored 10 of his 14 points inside the final minutes to lift the Cats to a 71–67 victory over UNCC.

Twice, Warford hit buckets that gave UK the upper hand, including a 15-footer that put the Cats in front for good at 64–63.

It was a fitting end for Warford, whose positive attitude, intelligence, and winning personality were instrumental in helping UK shed its all-white image.

For the season, Warford averaged 6.5 points per game.

7. Abraham Lincoln Collinsworth. Yes, you know his son, Cris. You see/hear him every week during the NFL season. He was a tremendous football player, and is currently one of the best analysts in the business.

The elder Collinsworth, who lettered three years at UK (1956–58), was born in Salyersville, Kentucky, on Abraham Lincoln's birthday (February 12). When Collinsworth arrived at UK, he was known as Lincoln. However, when Adolph Rupp began calling him Abe, the name stuck. He was never a big scorer, but he did make some valuable contributions on the 1957–58 team that won the NCAA title.

After graduating, Collinsworth spent his entire life as an educator, serving in virtually every capacity—teacher, coach, counselor, and principal. He eventually became superintendent of Brevard County (Florida) schools.

I have one clear and vivid memory of meeting Collinsworth when I was eleven years old. After the Fiddlin' Five team won the NCAA tourney, the seniors went on a barnstorming tour. One of the stops was at the Owensboro Sportscenter.

After the game, my cousin and I were standing with a group of fans outside the locker room. We were all waiting for the players to emerge, hoping to get autographs of our heroes. For whatever reason, I boldly knocked on the dressing room door, which was opened by Collinsworth, who immediately invited my cousin and me to come inside.

"But won't your boss get mad at you for letting us in?" I asked.

"I'm my own boss," Collinsworth said, grinning. "No one in here will get mad at anyone."

Thanks to him, we got autographs before anyone else did.

8. From a list that includes more than thirty names of players who guided their high school team to the state title, surely you came up with five. Here goes:

Burgess Carey, James McFarland, and Lovell Underwood—Lexington Lafayette (1922)

Ellis Johnson and Darrell Darby—Ashland (1928)

Dave Lawrence—Corinth (1930)

Marion Cluggish—Corbin (1936)

Jim King—Sharpe (1938)

Tom Moseley—Lexington Lafayette (1942)

Wah Wah Jones—Harlan (1944)

Ralph Beard—Male (1945)

Cliff Hagan—Owensboro (1949)

Linville Puckett—Clark County (1951)

Vernon Hatton—Lexington Lafayette (1953)
Billy Ray Cassady—Inez (1954)
Johnny Cox—Hazard (1955)
Billy Ray Lickert—Lexington Lafayette (1957)
Jim McDonald—Louisville St. Xavier (1958)
Pat Doyle—North Marshall (1959)
Ted Deeken—Louisville Flaget (1960)
Larry Conley—Ashland (1961)
Mike Casey and Bill Busey—Shelby County (1966)
Charles Hurt—Shelby County (1978)
Dirk Minniefield—Lexington Lafayette (1979)
Troy McKinley—Simon Kenton (1981)
Paul Andrews—Laurel County (1982)
Reggie Hanson—Pulaski County (1986)
Richie Farmer—Clay County (1987)
Anthony Epps—Marion County (1993)
Darius Miller—Mason County (2008)

9. Ralph Carlisle. Recognized as one of the premier prep coaches in Kentucky high school history, Carlisle pretty much had a machine at Lafayette during the 1950s, taking five teams to the Sweet 16 and winning three times. For his efforts, he was named that decade's Coach of the Year by the Louisville *Courier-Journal*.

Carlisle's overall record was 488–144. Among the many players he molded and developed are ex-Wildcat standouts Vernon Hatton and Billy

Ray Lickert, along with Charley Hadden, Bob Mulcahy, Jim Weiland, and Bill Florence.

Carlisle was no stranger to the Sweet 16, having twice led Kavanaugh High School to that tournament. He was named to the all-tournament team two times.

At UK, Carlisle was a two-time member of both the All-SEC team and the All-SEC Tournament team.

As a coach, Carlisle was demanding, to say the least, especially when it came to the fundamentals. His teams were known for being fundamentally sound.

"He was a drill sergeant in practice and a father figure off the court," Mulcahy said. "He always pushed his players to be the best players and the best people they could be."

When a sportswriter once asked the long-retired and somewhat cantankerous Carlisle if he would have liked to coach in the NBA, he quipped, "Not unless those guys were willing to learn the basic fundamentals of the game, which too many of them don't know. I wouldn't tolerate players who don't play the game the right way."

Adolph Rupp once called Carlisle the best high school coach in Kentucky.

10. Kenny Rollins and Dale Barnstable. During their run to the 1948 NCAA championship, the Wildcats—the Fabulous Five gang—had to

The powerful 1947–48 team. Sitting (l-r): Adolph Rupp, Johnny Stough, Ralph Beard, Kenny Rollins, Cliff Barker, Dale Barnstable, and assistant coach Harry Lancaster. Standing (l-r): manager Humzey Yessin, Garland Townes, Jim Jordan, Joe Holland, Alex Groza, Wah Wah Jones, Jim Line, Roger Day, and trainer Bud Berger.
Photo courtesy of University of Kentucky Athletics.

get past Holy Cross in the semifinal game. That meant going up against the great Bob Cousy.

Holy Cross came into this game with a 25–3 record and a 19-game winning streak. Pretty good, yes, but the Cats entered the contest with a 34–3 mark. Simply put, this was a true showdown between a pair of outstanding teams.

With the score knotted at 7–7, the Cats, a five-point favorite, rode an early scoring outburst by

Ralph Beard to break the deadlock and seize control of the game. When it was all over, the Cats prevailed 60–52.

Alex Groza paced the winners with 23 points, while Beard and Wah Wah Jones chipped in with 13 and 12, respectively.

Rollins, UK's Minister of Defense, with occasional relief from Barnstable, limited Cousy to one field goal and three free throws for a total of five points. Cousy came into the contest averaging just under 20 points per game.

The championship game against Baylor was almost anticlimactic. The Cats jumped out to a 24–7 lead and then went on to win it 58–42. Groza, the tourney MVP, led the Cats with 14 points. Beard had 12, Rollins and Jones nine apiece.

This would be the first of back-to-back NCAA titles by Rupp's Wildcats. One year later they repeated by beating Oklahoma A&M 46–36 in the title game.

11. The 1953–54 team. This is the team led by Cliff Hagan, Frank Ramsey, and Lou Tsioropoulos that went 25–0 and then didn't play in the NCAA Tournament. Also, keep in mind that this team beat La Salle, the eventual NCAA champs, 73–60 in the UKIT.

The average margin of victory was 27.2 points, and incredibly, only two teams played the Cats to within 10 points.

One of those teams was powerful LSU. Led by All-American Bob Pettit, the Tigers, like UK, ended the season with a 14–0 SEC record. Because of a scheduling disagreement, the two teams had not faced each other during the regular season. Therefore, a one-game playoff was scheduled to be played in Nashville. The winner would be crowned SEC champs and earn a trip to the NCAA Tournament.

Ramsey was the difference in this one, erupting for 30 points to lead the Cats to a 63–56 victory. Hagan and Pettit, future teammates on the St. Louis Hawks, each had 17 points.

It wasn't long after this game that word got out that Hagan, Ramsey, and Tsioropoulos couldn't participate in the NCAA tourney because they were graduate students. Although the nine other players voted to go forward without that trio, Adolph Rupp quickly laid that notion to rest. The Baron wasn't about to go anywhere without those three.

Many years later, Ramsey told Cawood Ledford that after the vote, Rupp came back into the locker room and said, "We're not going, because I'm not going to take a bunch of turds like you to the NCAA."

Verdict delivered, case closed.

12. Dan Issel, Jack Givens, and Tayshaun Prince. During the 1970 NCAA Mideast Regional, Issel scored 44 points in a difficult 109–99 victory over ninth-ranked Notre Dame. Believe it or not, Issel was not the game's high scorer. That honor

Tayshaun Prince prepares to head for the bucket.
Photo courtesy of David Coyle.

went to Irish All-American Austin Carr, who torched the Cats for 52 points.

Givens scored 41 points in the Cats' 94–88 win over Duke in the 1978 title game. He blistered Duke's zone defense, racking up 16 of UK's final 18 first-half points en route to a 45–38 lead at the break. In the second half, whenever it looked like the Blue Devils might take command, Givens shattered those hopes by consistently knocking down big buckets.

As the *Sports Illustrated* cover said: The Goose was Golden.

Giving the most-remarkable performance of his career, Prince gunned in 41 points to lead the Cats past stubborn Tulsa 87–82 in second-round action in 2002. Prince made good on 14 of 21 field goal attempts, including six of eight from beyond the three-point arc. He accounted for 28 of UK's final 46 first-half points, and then in the second half, with Tulsa hanging close at 51–47, he continued to knock down long-range jumpers that helped his team survive and advance. Prince, like Givens, was a lefty.

13. C. M. Newton. His first coaching stop was at Transylvania College, where he remained for ten years. Next, he spent twelve years at Alabama, then eight more at Vanderbilt. His overall NCAA coaching record is 509–375.

Newton's 1971–72 Alabama team beat the Wildcats 73–70 in Tuscaloosa, marking the first time an ex-player defeated a UK squad.

His Alabama teams would top UK on several occasions during his tenure, a feat only one of his Vanderbilt teams could manage.

He has served as SEC commissioner, president of USA Basketball, and UK athletics director. It was Newton who hired Rick Pitino to rebuild the scandal-marred program.

As a player at UK, Newton only scored 27 points in his two years, but he did have one game where his play made a difference. Facing Illinois in the 1951 East Regional title game, Newton's defense shut down Illini star guard Don Sunderlage, which helped the Cats slip by 76–74. This UK team went on the claim the NCAA title.

Perhaps more than anyone else, Newton is responsible for opening the SEC to black athletes. When Alabama AD Paul "Bear" Bryant offered him the job, Newton said he would do it on one condition—there were no limitations when it came to recruiting. Bryant didn't hesitate, giving Newton the go-ahead to recruit the best players, regardless of color.

Vanderbilt was the first SEC school to sign a black player, but it was Newton who really opened the doors that forever changed—and improved—the Southeastern Conference. And he did it at time when the Grand Wizard of the Ku Klux Klan still had an office at the end of University Avenue.

During a UK practice, Adolph Rupp, frustrated by Newton's performance in a scrimmage game,

Adolph Rupp with former Wildcat C. M. Newton, then the coach at Alabama.

Photo courtesy of University of Kentucky Athletics.

pulled him off the court and said, "You know what you remind me of? A Shetland pony in a stud horse parade."

While C. M. Newton might not rank among UK's all-time greatest players, he does rank at the very top when it comes to things like character, class, decency, and honor. He's in the Basketball Hall of Fame, and he certainly deserves to be.

14. Shawn Kemp and Enes Kanter. There are some who will tell you that to this very day Kemp is the most talented player to ever sign a UK scholarship. In preseason pickup games he dominated everyone, including Kenny Walker, then an NBA player. Kemp was a genuinely great talent.

He played for Concord High School in Elkhart, Indiana. In 1988, he was a member of a strong McDonald's All-America team that included Alonzo Mourning, Chris Mills, Billy Owens, Lee Mayberry, Anthony Peeler, and Stanley Roberts.

Kemp failed to meet the required SAT score, which meant he had to sit out his freshman season. Then, in November, he was accused of pawning two gold chains that had reportedly been stolen from Sean Sutton. Although no criminal charges were filed, Kemp decided to leave UK.

Following a brief stint at Trinity Valley Community College in Texas, Kemp declared himself eligible for the NBA draft. He was chosen in the first round by Seattle. In all, Kemp played 14 seasons in the NBA. His best year was in 1998–99 when he averaged 20.5 points for Cleveland.

Kanter, who grew to 6'11", was born in Zurich, Switzerland, but grew up in Turkey. He moved to the US in 2009 and enrolled at Stoneridge Preparatory School in Simi Valley, California, where he immediately grabbed the attention of every big-time college coach.

During his senior season, he verbally committed to play for the Washington Huskies. But by the next spring, he changed his mind and opened the recruiting process again. In April he signed with UK.

That's when the NCAA decided to step in. After a lengthy process, the NCAA ruled Kanter permanently ineligible because he had been paid $33,000 in excess fees while playing on professional-level teams in Turkey. UK appealed the NCAA's ruling, but to no avail. The appeal was rejected.

Kanter was drafted third overall by Utah in the 2011 NBA draft. After playing three-plus seasons there, he was traded to Oklahoma City. In his first full year with the Thunder, he scored at an 18.7 clip.

Had either Kemp or Kanter played at UK, both would have been first-team All-Americans. You can take that to the bank.

15. Bennie Coffman. If you're searching for a game the Wildcats had no business winning, then look no further than their 1958 game against Maryland in Memorial Coliseum. This is one the Cats absolutely should not have won.

The scoreboard told the story: Maryland 54, UK 51, 10 seconds remaining. Local sportswriters were already busy composing UK's obituary. A rare home-court loss was inevitable.

During a timeout, the two coaches—one desperate, the other virtually certain of victory—mapped entirely different strategies.

UK's Adolph Rupp: "I told them we had to drive for a basket, and had to get fouled at the same time. One basket wouldn't do us any good. It was to be either Coffman or [Dickie] Parsons."

Maryland's Bud Millikan: "I told the boys to let Kentucky pass the ball in and go ahead and score. We'd still have possession of the ball and time would run out before we would have to put it in play."

Rupp's prayers for a miracle were heard; Millikan's call for common sense fell on deaf ears.

As planned, Coffman ended up with the ball. He drove through the middle of Maryland's defense, laid in a bucket, and, incredibly, drew a foul on Al Bunge, who, for some unknown reason, attempted to block the shot. Coffman converted the free throw to send the game into overtime and give the Wildcats new life.

Bennie Coffman, one heck of a miracle worker.
Photo courtesy of University of Kentucky Athletics.

In overtime, after Johnny Cox nailed a one-hander from the side to give UK a 56–54 lead, the two teams went scoreless for the next three minutes. Following a Maryland miss, the Wildcats froze the ball until Parsons was fouled with 34 seconds remaining. He sank both free tosses to make it 58–54. Maryland's Jim Halleck hit two free throws, but it was too little, too late.

UK escaped with a 58–56 victory.

Cox had a big game for the winners, scoring 18 points and snaring 14 rebounds. Billy Ray Lickert finished with 16 points, while Coffman, the hero, tossed in 10.

After the game, Maryland coach Millikan could only shake his head at what had just transpired. "I told them not to foul, but to get out of the way if Kentucky drove," Millikan lamented. "They did just the opposite."

16. Dr. David Roselle. Even now, many UK fans have a decidedly mixed opinion of Roselle for the way he handled things following the scandal that erupted during Eddie Sutton's time as Wildcat coach. Those who view Roselle as something of a Judas think he caved to the NCAA more than he should have, while others see him as the guy who cleaned up a dirty program.

In his autobiography, Cawood Ledford caught the waves from both sides of the ocean. "I think David Roselle was a well-meaning, good man, but I also think he was the most naïve college president ever involved in an

NCAA investigation. He brought in an outside investigator and ordered him to conduct an investigation that was far, far more thorough than anything the NCAA had ever done or could do. He gave him access to everything.

"I think Roselle was hoping that by doing it that way, the NCAA would be lenient. Instead, the penalties that were finally handed down—two years' ineligibility for the NCAA Tournament and no live TV for a year were the crux of it—were about as severe as they could be. I had a lawyer, a guy who had studied all the evidence tell me that if UK had fought the NCAA, the program would have only gotten a slap on the wrist.

"But in fairness, I'll also say this for Roselle: He purged the program. Today it's one of the cleanest in the country and I don't think it might have been at that time."

Roselle became UK president on July 1, 1987. During his time in charge, he hired C. M. Newton as UK's athletics director, a move with profound and positive results that reverberate to this day.

Roselle resigned from UK in 1989.

17. UK vs. Phillips 66ers. This game took place at Madison Square Garden during the 1948 Olympic trials. It was the final game of the trials, with the winning team's coach being named the head coach of the US Olympic squad. The losing coach would be the assistant.

The five starters from each team, along with four other players, would represent the US in those game played in London. UK's starters were, of course, the Fabulous Five—Ralph Beard, Wah Wah Jones, Alex Groza, Kenny Rollins, and Cliff Barker.

The game was close and hotly contested from start to finish. With 18,475 fans looking on, the 66ers edged the Wildcats 53–49. To earn the victory, the 66ers had to overcome Beard's marvelous 23-point performance.

Beard had to carry a team that was hampered by the early departure of Barker (broken nose) and Jones (fouls). Barker suffered his injury midway through the first half, while Jones, the Cats' chief rebounder, fouled out in the final 20 minutes.

With Beard leading the charge, UK bolted to a 20–13 lead with eight minutes left in the first half. But the 66ers, sparked by seven-foot center Bob Kurland, answered with an 11–0 run that put them on top 24–20. The halftime score was 26–26.

Things remained tight in the final half. With just over six minutes remaining, Beard racked up a three-point play that put UK in front 47–45. That would be the last time UK held the upper hand.

Eight unanswered points by the 66ers gave them the lead for good. UK's Dale Barnstable banked in a short shot to account for the final 53–49 score.

Kurland had a big game on both ends of the court, scoring 20 points while holding high-scoring Groza to one field goal and four points.

After the game, 66ers coach Bud Browning said, "That's the greatest team we faced all year. And that little Beard. He is absolutely the best I ever saw."

As you might expect, losing coach Adolph Rupp wasn't in such a complimentary mood, telling his players, "I want to thank you very much for making me an assistant coach for the first time in my life."

18. Russell Rice. Anyone who writes a single word about UK's long and magnificent basketball history owes a huge debt of gratitude to Russell Rice. Without question, he is the preeminent historian of UK hoops and football. No one before him brought it all together like he did.

He had served as sports editor for the *Lexington Leader* before taking the job as sports information director at UK. It was under his watch that the sports information department became one of the best—and most influential—in the country. Yet, regardless of how big the department became, under Rice it always had a family feeling to it.

Adolph Rupp was coaching when Rice took over at UK. Later, he worked with Joe B. Hall, Eddie Sutton, Rick Pitino, and Tubby Smith.

Rice wrote several books about UK basketball, including a biography of Rupp, *The Wildcat*

Legacy and *Joe B. Hall: My Own Kentucky Home*.

However, his towering achievement is the classic *Big Blue Machine*, which gave a close-up look at UK hoops from the beginning through the time the book was published in 1976.

This book you are reading now, like all books about UK basketball, owes its lifeblood to the pioneering work Russell Rice did in the past. He is the starting point from which we all travel.

19. **Dr. Otis Singletary.** Adolph Rupp turned seventy, the mandatory retirement age for UK employees, during the 1971–72 campaign. With that, the stage was set for a showdown between the UK president and a legendary coach who had been at the helm since 1930.

Throughout the season, Rupp refused to acknowledge that it would be his final year as UK coach. Because of the swirling controversy the team's on-court accomplishments were overshadowed by the debate concerning Rupp's future. Would he be forced to retire, or would an exception be made in his case?

While Rupp remained fairly silent on the issue, it was no secret that behind closed doors he was marshaling his forces for the battle against Singletary. Rupp worked through the media, hoping to win the public's support. There were also petitions signed by former players and prominent Kentuckians arguing that Rupp should be allowed to remain as UK's coach.

For his part, Dr. Singletary made it clear that Rupp would not be granted any special favors. The battle lines had been drawn.

Caught in the middle of all this was Joe B. Hall, the man viewed by many as the logical successor to Rupp. Hall had played for Rupp, and was currently his assistant coach. It was Hall who upgraded UK's recruiting, and he was the force behind the shattering of the color barrier.

Despite what was clearly an uncomfortable situation for everyone concerned, the 1971–72 team finished with a 21–7 record, won the SEC championship, and ended up ranked No. 18 in the final polls.

When the smoke cleared, it was Dr. Singletary who had the last word—Rupp had to retire. A few weeks later, after the season ended, it was officially announced that Hall would be the new UK coach. At the press conference introducing Hall, Rupp was conspicuous by his absence.

Singletary once confided to Cawood Ledford that when he took over as UK president and was going over everyone's salary, he was stunned to see that Rupp was only making in the neighborhood of $19,500 per year. Singletary couldn't believe his eyes. Rupp, the man who had won more games than any coach, who had led his teams to four NCAA championships, and who, because of Wildcat basketball success, had given Kentuckians something to be proud of, was receiving such a paltry salary. Singletary immediately increased Rupp's salary to $32,000.

Think about that the next time you hear of a coach demanding and getting a multiyear, multimillion dollar contract. Then just for good measure, compare that coach's accomplishments against Rupp's. Makes you wonder just how much Rupp would be worth these days, doesn't it?

20. Adolph Rupp, Joe B. Hall, Cawood Ledford, Rick Pitino, and Bill Keightley. Rupp, Hall, and Pitino were, of course, head coaches responsible for six of the school's eight national championships. (Hall was also a player, but his banner is in recognition of his coaching accomplishments.)

Cawood (no one *ever* referred to him as Mr. Ledford) was the "Voice of the Wildcats" for thirty-nine seasons, during which he proved to be among the very best, if not *the* best play-by-play announcer in the business. He was so good that when a UK game was televised, many Wildcat fans turned down the TV volume and listened to Cawood's call. Those who did never ceased to be amazed at how on the money he was while calling the action.

Cawood called UK football games during those thirty-nine years, and from 1961 until the early 1980s, he also called horse racing, including the Kentucky Derby on many occasions. He always maintained that calling horse races was the most challenging gig of them all.

Keightley, "Mr. Wildcat," spent five decades serving as UK equipment manager, friend, confidant, and father confessor to virtually every Wildcat player who put on the uniform during all those years. If a player was slumping, down in the dumps, feeling blue or homesick, Keightley was the guy they vented their frustrations to. And the guy who always managed to make them feel better.

Here are the answers to the five multiple choice questions:

21. (c) John Mauer. He coached at UK for three seasons (1928–30) and actually had some success. His three UK teams had a combined record of 40–14, which computes to a winning percentage of .741.

Before Mauer took over, the longest tenure of any previous UK coach belonged to George Buchheit, who held the position from 1920 to 1924. Mostly, though, in those early years, coaches usually didn't hang around much longer than a year.

Mauer had been a standout player at the University of Illinois prior to getting into the coaching business. Coming to UK, he brought with him a deliberate, controlled "submarine" attack that consisted primarily of bounce passes and steady movement. Mauer was strict, organized, and focused, and his style of play was new and somewhat mystifying to his players.

At the time, most offenses designated certain players for specific roles. Mauer's plan was radically different. He incorporated all five players into the attack, giving equal importance to guards, forwards, and centers.

It could be argued—and rightfully so—that Mauer brought an element to UK basketball that was more important than wins and losses. He brought a demand for excellence. He was a tough, demanding coach who expected his players to take a serious approach to the game.

Basketball, under Mauer, developed into something more than a disorganized game played by a ragtag group of players. It was a game played with logic, precision, and structure.

Mauer became, according to the school newspaper, the "Moses" who led the sport out of the wilderness and into the dawn of a new era.

Mauer's tenure happened to coincide with an influx of new and talented players, including two—Carey Spicer and Paul McBrayer—who earned All-America recognition.

Mauer left UK after the 1929–30 campaign to take a similar job at Miami (Ohio) University. Later, he would become the head coach at Tennessee, where he would go up against his successor, Adolph Rupp, a coach who brought with him an entirely different style of basketball. And Mauer would win his share of those games.

22. (b) Bob Burrow. All four of these guys came from the JUCO ranks, but Burrow was the first, arriving at UK in 1955. Burrow couldn't have

showed up at a better time. With the great Cliff Hagan having graduated the previous season, the 6'7" Burrow was being counted on to provide scoring, rebounding, and interior defense for the Wildcats.

Burrow didn't disappoint anyone. In his two seasons at UK, he scored 1,023 points and grabbed 823 rebounds. He once scored 50 points in a game and pulled down 34 rebounds in another game. His career scoring average was 20.1, and his 16.1 rebounds per game is UK's all-time career best. He was twice voted onto the All-SEC team, and in 1956, he was a second-team All-America selection.

Smith, nicknamed "Odie" after a comedian on the Grand Ole Opry, played his prep ball at Farmington (Kentucky) High School, but not before the principal/coach agreed to give him a ride home (seven miles) after practices. Smith only received one scholarship offer (Murray State), but he waited too long to accept, so the offer was withdrawn.

He spent two years at Northeast Mississippi Junior College, where he acquitted himself well enough that Adolph Rupp offered him a scholarship to UK. This time Smith didn't take too long to sign on the dotted line.

As a junior during the 1956–57 season, Smith didn't see much action until Vernon Hatton was sidelined because of an appendectomy. Smith made the most of his opportunity, averaging 16.3 points in those seven games.

As a senior and a member of the Fiddlin' Five, Smith averaged 12.4 points and helped that team win the 1958 NCAA championship.

In the summer of 1960, Smith was on the US Olympic team that many still consider the greatest of all time. That team included such legends as Oscar Robertson, Jerry West, and Jerry Lucas. To no one's surprise, that team waltzed to the gold medal.

Smith played many years in the NBA, and in 1966 he was named the All-Star game MVP after scoring 24 points in 26 minutes.

Cohen, a Brooklyn native, came to UK after playing two seasons at Kilgore (Texas) Junior College, where he led his team to JUCO championships in 1957 and 1958. He was twice named MVP.

Cohen actually came to Adolph Rupp's attention while playing on the US Army European team that won the 1955 championships. Rupp was conducting a basketball clinic in Germany when he first became aware of him. After seeing Cohen in action in Germany and at Kilgore Junior College, Rupp offered him a UK scholarship.

Cohen played two years at UK, scoring a total of 471 points. He averaged 8.1 points as a junior in 1958–59 and 10.7 as senior the next year.

As Russell Rice recounted in his book *Big Blue Machine,* during one practice session, Rupp was displeased with the way Cohen was running the offense. In particular, Rupp wasn't happy because Cohen kept working the ball away from a certain player. Finally, Rupp blew his whistle, walked out onto the court, and addressed Cohen.

"Sidney," Rupp said, "I want you to meet Johnny Cox of Hazard, Kentucky. He's working over on that side of the court. He's a pretty good basketball player. He just won the national championship for us last year. But he won't have a chance to do it again this year unless you let him feel the ball once in a while. Sidney, I would appreciate it very much if you would pass the ball to Johnny."

Cohen was drafted in the fourth round by the NBA's Boston Celtics.

Coffman, hero of that Maryland game, came to UK after playing for Lindsey Wilson Junior College. At UK, he performed with great consistency, averaging 10.7 as a junior and 10.2 in his final season. In all, this native of Huntington, West Virginia, scored 526 points as a Wildcat.

23. (b) Ed Beck. Although never a big scorer, the 6'7" Beck was a solid rebounder and defender. He was a two-year starter in the pivot, averaging 9.5 points as a junior and 5.6 on the 1958 NCAA championship club. During his junior season, he snagged 14.1 rebounds per game.

For his career, Beck scored 459 points and had 783 rebounds. After the 1957–58 season he was named SEC Defensive Player of the Year.

No doubt, he had played that season with a heavy heart, having tragically lost his wife, Billie, to cancer at the end of the previous season.

Pursiful is associate pastor at Westport Road Baptist Church in Louisville, and Mills is a well-respected speaker and founder of the non-profit Cameron Mills Ministries.

Rollins was recognized as having a beautiful singing voice, and was often asked to showcase his great talent in a variety of venues.

24. (b) Roger Newman. In his final game, an 87–74 loss to powerful Ohio State, Newman made good on 17 of 22 free throws in a strong 31-point performance. Those 17 free tosses are the most by a Wildcat during NCAA tourney action.

Dwight Anderson holds the single-game mark with 18 against Mississippi State, while Cliff Hagan owns the record for most free throws attempted in a game—24 against Temple.

Newman's journey—his odyssey, really—is quite an interesting one. This Greenville (Kentucky) High School star was one of the top four players in a very strong 1956 senior class, along with Wayland's "King" Kelly Coleman, Central City's Corky Withrow, and Berea's Don Mills. All were high on Adolph Rupp's wish list. He did manage to land three of the four. Only Coleman said no to a UK scholarship offer.

Joining that trio was Jackie Moreland, a 6'7" lefty from Minden, Louisiana, who scored 5,030 points, still fourth-best in US prep history. Getting Moreland made this arguably the strongest class Rupp had ever recruited. Surely, Wildcat fans couldn't wait to see these four standouts wearing UK blue and white.

But it all unraveled rather quickly. Withrow, another natural scorer with more than 3,100 points to his credit, signed a baseball contract with the Milwaukee Braves in midsummer, thus making him ineligible at UK. In those days, no pro athlete could participate in any Division I sport. He would go on to score more than 1,200 points in two seasons at Georgetown (Kentucky) College.

Moreland's situation turned out to be on the mysterious side. According to Russell Rice, when school began in the fall, Moreland's trunk arrived with his clothes but he didn't. He'd gone missing. What happened? Well, seems he'd been highjacked by another school—North Carolina State, whose coach was Everett Case, a man Rupp was not particularly fond of.

Moreland kept changing his mind, but he also kept assuring Rupp and Harry Lancaster that he had every intention of honoring his commitment to UK. Meanwhile, he also committed to Texas A&M and Centenary before finally signing with N.C. State.

But Moreland never played a game for the Wolfpack, and the school was put on probation for allegedly offering him cash and gifts if he signed. Moreland left N.C. State and transferred to Louisiana Tech, where he scored 1,419 points.

The 6'7" Mills stayed at UK all four years and had a solid career. He was a backup center—and valuable contributor—on the 1957–58 NCAA championship team, then was a starter his final two seasons, averaging 10.5 points as a junior and 12.7 as a senior. For his career, Mills, an All-SEC selection as a senior, scored 664 points and had 669 rebounds.

That brings us back to Newman, who some might argue was the best all-around athlete of the quartet. He could score, defend, and rebound. One of his strengths was excellent leaping ability. Newman was also a good shooter who became an even better one when he began wearing glasses.

Newman came to UK and played his freshman season. Then for myriad reasons, he left UK and began three years in exile. In 1960, after wandering in the basketball wasteland, he came back to UK. And in what would be his only season he showed just how much UK fans had missed out on.

Despite three full years of inactivity, Newman was the second-leading scorer (14.1) on that 1960–61 team, and although only 6'4", he was the leading rebounder (9.5). He scored 20 points in his first varsity game (a UK best at the time), had one four-game stretch in which he rang up 92 points, including 26 in a win over UCLA, and then closed out his career with those 31 points against Ohio State, with its terrific trio of Jerry Lucas, John Havlicek, and Larry Siegfried.

One can only speculate as to what Newman might have achieved had he played all three seasons as a Wildcat.

25. (c) Cliff Barker. All four of these ex-Cats nailed shots from long distance, but Barker wins the prize. This magician with a basketball apparently had long-range accuracy as well. During a 1949 game against Vanderbilt at the old Alumni Gym, Barker hit one that was later measured at 63'7". In case you're wondering, that's well past the midcourt stripe.

The second spot goes to Ralph Beard, who hit one from 53'9" against Tennessee in 1948.

Third on the long-distance list is Linville Puckett, who scored from 53'6" away against Mississippi State in 1954.

Of the four longest field goals, the most important was the one made by Joe "Red" Hagan in 1938 against Marquette. With the score tied at 33–33, Hagan dropped in a bomb from 48'2" to give the Wildcats a thrilling victory. It was after this game that Kentucky governor Happy Chandler pounded a nail into the floor to mark the spot where Hagan had launched his game-deciding shot.

Of course, no list of long shots would be complete without mentioning what was perhaps the most memorable of all—Vernon Hatton's desperation bucket from 47 feet away against Temple that tied the game at the end of the first overtime and kept alive the Wildcats' chances for victory, which they achieved with an 85–83 triple-overtime win.

4

HALL OF FAME LEVEL

(Answers begin on Page 150)

1. Who did UK's first win come against?

2. What UK team was the first to win a major tournament?

3. Who scored the first basket in Adolph Rupp's initial game as UK's head coach?

4. What Wildcat later became a successful character actor on such TV series as *The Deputy*, *Gunsmoke*, and *Bonanza*, and in such movies as *Kelly's Heroes* and *Maverick*?

5. Name the UK player who was involved in a midcourt fistfight with an opponent during pregame warmups.

6. Who are the only three Wildcats to earn All-SEC first-team and All-SEC Tournament first-team honors all four years they played?

7. Name the five former Wildcat players who paid the ultimate price during World War II.

8. Who was the opponent's leading scorer in Adolph Rupp's first game at UK?

9. Four Wildcats grabbed more than 1,000 rebounds during their playing days. Who are they?

10. Who scored the first points for a John Calipari–coached Wildcat team?

11. What did the superstitious Adolph Rupp consider to be a sign of good luck if he found them on the ground as he headed toward Memorial Coliseum prior to a game?

12. What world class violinist gave a concert at Memorial Coliseum that forced an irate Adolph Rupp to move practice to the old Alumni Gym?

13. Who was the first ex-Cat to play on an NBA championship team?

14. What former Wildcat basketball player also played baseball and was signed by the mighty New York Yankees?

15. Name the sportswriter who broke the news that Cliff Hagan, Frank Ramsey, and Lou Tsioropoulos were fifth-year seniors, thus making them ineligible to participate in the NCAA Tournament.

HALL OF FAME ANSWERS

1. On February 18, 1903, UK, then known as Kentucky State College, edged the Lexington YMCA 11–10 for the first of the school's more than 2,200 victories. The Cadets, the team's nickname in those days, finished the season with a 1–2 record, wrapping losses to Georgetown (Kentucky) College and Kentucky University (now Transylvania College) around that lone win.

    The first basketball team was put together by Walter W. H. Mustaine, the school's physical education director. Most of the players were members of the football team. Mustaine took up a collection totaling three dollars to pay for the ball, then told the boys to find some uniforms and shoes, elect a captain, and begin playing.

    Such was the modest beginning of the winningest program of all-time, one Rick

Pitino would later call "the Roman Empire of college basketball."

Members of that first team included H. J. Wurtele, J. White Guyn, Joe Coons, R. H. Arnett, Leander Andrus, William Goodwin, Harold Amoss, J. Cronley Elliott, Ed Pierce, and G. C. Montgomery.

UK posted a losing record in each of the first six seasons the school fielded a basketball team. That didn't change until the 1908–09 team finished with a 5–4 mark.

Although Mustaine was the chief overseer, those early teams were run by student managers, while the task of actually coaching the squad fell to the elected captain. The manager of that first winning team was J. S. Chambers; the captain was W. C. Fox.

The school's first true coach was E. R. Sweetland, a native of Dryden, New York, and a former standout athlete at Cornell University. But Sweetland turned out to be something of a gypsy. He coached part of the 1909–10 season, then left Kentucky because of poor health. He returned two years later and coached one more season before packing his bag and departing Kentucky for good.

It really wasn't until George Buchheit arrived in 1920 that a measure of stability settled on the basketball program. Buchheit stayed on the job for five seasons. Between the time Sweetland left for good and Buchheit's arrival, six different men held down the coaching position.

2. The 1920–21 team coached by Buchheit slipped past Georgia 20–19 to win the Southern Intercollegiate Athletic Association Tournament in Atlanta. It was a game filled with tension, excitement, and plenty of game-ending drama.

On their way to the title showdown, the Wildcats marched through the first three games like Sherman heading toward Atlanta. In those easy romps, the Cats whipped Tulane 50–28, Mercer 49–25, and Mississippi A&M 28–13 to set up the championship battle against Georgia.

And boy, was that game a doozy. The game was a tense and close struggle all the way, with the Cats holding an 8–7 lead at intermission. After a seesaw second half, the Bulldogs finally managed to take a 19–17 lead with a little more than a minute left to play.

Moments later, UK's Basil Hayden got free and scored a bucket to tie it at 19–19 with 45 ticks remaining. Don't forget, in those days there was a jump ball after every made basket. It was a rule that worked to UK's advantage on this night.

On the ensuing center jump, UK's Bobby Lavin came up with the ball and then fired a pass to teammate Paul Adkins near the bucket. As Adkins went up for a sure two points, he was fouled hard by a Georgia player.

Back then, one player was usually designated to shoot all of his team's free throws. For UK, that was Bill King. Also, the clock didn't stop while a player was attempting a free throw.

However, the game couldn't end until the player finished shooting.

As King lifted his arms to shoot, just as the clock ticked down to zero, the timer's pistol was discharged. With the crowd now deathly silent, King, ignoring the distraction, fired his free toss. The ball hit the rim, eased slightly to the right, then fell through, giving the Wildcats a one-point win and the tourney title.

The Wildcats finished that season with a 13–1 record.

Hundreds of adoring fans were on hand to meet the triumphant Wildcats when they arrived back in Lexington. This was the first time UK fans celebrated a championship with their conquering Big Blue heroes. It would not be the last.

3. Aggie Sale. In UK's 67–19 win over Georgetown (Kentucky) College, Sale, a sophomore, led all scorers with 19 points. That initial bucket by Sale sent the Wildcats off and running in what would be the first of new coach Adolph Rupp's 876 career victories.

    Rupp's arrival, along with his more up-tempo style of play, was a perfect fit for Sale, who, at 6'5", could score, rebound, and defend. In many ways it could be said that Sale was UK's first "modern" All-American. In an era when there weren't many high-scoring players, Sale was certainly an exception.

He went over the 20-point mark on multiple occasions during his three years as a starter, a span in which the Wildcats had an overall record of 51–8. Those three years, and the next two, really set the tone for UK's great basketball success.

As a junior, Sale scored 21 against Tulane and 20 against both Washington & Lee and North Carolina. In his final season, he accounted for 73 points in four games to help the Wildcats win the inaugural SEC Tournament. In that tournament, he had back-to-back 20-point efforts against Florida and LSU.

Sale averaged 5.6 as a sophomore, 13.6 as a junior, and 13.8 as a senior. His final two seasons, he teamed with Frenchy DeMoisey, another prolific scorer, to give the Wildcats an extremely potent inside tandem.

In 1933, Sale was named the Helms Foundation National Player of the Year.

Sale was UK's fifth All-American, and like the four who came before him he was a Kentucky kid. In fact, UK's first seven All-America selections were in-state guys. Basil Hayden was from Paris, Burgess Carey and Carey Spicer were from Lexington, Paul McBrayer and Sale hailed from Lawrenceburg, Ellis Johnson came from Ashland, and DeMoisey was from Walton.

It wouldn't be until 1935 when Indianapolis native Leroy Edwards earned the honor that the Kentucky-only All-American lineage was finally broken.

4. Read Morgan. There is a pretty good chance that you've never heard of Read Morgan, but there is virtually a 100 percent chance that you've seen him. If you attend movies or watch TV, you can count on having watched something he was in. Although only a character actor, he has been seen in more than 140 movies and TV series. From the mid-1950s until the mid-1990s, he was steadily employed in a business that is known for having a notoriously high unemployment rate.

Morgan came to UK from Chicago and was on the team for two seasons, although he never earned a letter. He very well might have been a good basketball player, but at UK in those days (early 1950s), being good wasn't enough. A player had to be outstanding if he hoped to see action. With guys like Bill Spivey, Cliff Hagan, Frank Ramsey, Bobby Watson, Lou Tsioropoulos, Jim Line, Walt Hirsch, and Skippy Whitaker on the roster, it's easy to see why Morgan didn't get much playing time.

After leaving UK, Morgan began his acting career, first on Broadway as an athletic mountaineer in *Li'l Abner*. His TV debut came in 1956 when he appeared as a wrestler in two episodes on the *United States Steel Hour*.

His longest-running gig was as the patch-wearing "Sarge" on *The Deputy*, starring the legendary Henry Fonda. He appeared in seemingly every TV series at least once, and along with *Kelly's Heroes* and *Maverick*, other films of his include *Back to the Future* and *Dillinger*.

Morgan also wrote the foreword for the book, *Henry Fonda and the Deputy: The Film and Stage Star and His TV Western.*

His final role was as a card dealer in *Maverick* (1994).

Here's a great story C. M. Newton told me about Read Morgan. Keep in mind that C. M. and Morgan were on the team at the same time.

Since Morgan was hardly seeing any action at all, Adolph Rupp decided it was time to cut him from the team. Word was sent to Morgan that he was to be at Rupp's office at a designated time. Cutting a player from the team is never an easy thing to do, so Rupp, not wanting to deliver bad news alone, ask assistant coach Harry Lancaster to join him for the meeting.

However, before the meeting took place, Morgan got wind of what was about to happen. Thanks to the person who leaked the information, Morgan didn't go into the meeting unprepared. When Morgan showed up, Rupp and Lancaster were sitting there, ready to inform him that his basketball services were no longer needed.

But they never got the chance, because when Morgan entered the office, he immediately said, "Coach Rupp, I'm here to let you know that I'm quitting the team. I have no further interest in playing basketball. Instead, I'm going to concentrate on my acting career. What this means is that the next time you see me perform, you'll have to pay to get in just like everyone else."

With that, Morgan did an about-face and walked out, leaving Rupp sitting there silent, flabbergasted, and totally one-upped.

Hats off to Read Morgan for being one of the very few who managed to get in the last word on Adolph Rupp.

5. Dan Chandler. In the annals of UK basketball history this certainly has to rank as perhaps the most bizarre incident ever. Yes, fights during the game happen all the time. We've all seen dozens of them. Players have been known to engage in fights after a game, or occasionally even when heading for the locker room at halftime.

But a pregame altercation? That's just *never* happens.

Only it did, proving again that one should never say never.

On a cold February night in 1955, the Wildcats were taking on Alabama at Memorial Coliseum. While it may have been frosty outside, it wasn't long before the action inside heated up.

In those days, during warmups five or six players would be shooting while the rest of the players stood out around the midcourt line waiting until their time came to fire up a few shots. Chandler was one of the UK players standing at midcourt.

Apparently, Chandler didn't like the way Bama's Jim Bogan was looking at him, so the feisty Chandler dared Bogan to step over the line. Bogan did and Chandler went after him.

Although Chandler was at a distinct size disadvantage—the tale of the tape would list him at 5'10" and Bogan at 6'7"—the decision was unanimous. Chandler was declared the fight's clear-cut winner by the many sportswriters who witnessed the brawl.

Chandler, son of Happy Chandler, played two seasons at UK, racking up a grand total of 10 points. He later became a well-known casino executive in Las Vegas and Lake Tahoe. Later in his career, Chandler, who was something of a Damon Runyon–type character, had the job of entertaining what are known as "whales," those very wealthy individuals who come to the casinos willing to spend thousands—even millions—of dollars in a very brief period of time. Chandler's task was to ensure that those folks received even better than VIP treatment.

And he was certainly well-suited for the job. Chandler was colorful, brash, a loud talker and full of BS, but he always had that twinkle in his eyes. If you needed his help, all you had to do was ask.

6. Jack Tingle, Ralph Beard, and Wah Wah Jones. The guess here is you named Beard and Jones, but stumbled when it came to Tingle. That's not surprising, since Tingle seldom gets the recognition—or appreciation—he deserves.

All three of these guys benefited from the time in which they played. Because World War II wreaked havoc with so many team rosters, the

NCAA bent the rules and allowed players to be on the varsity squad for all four years. At the end of the 1948–49 season, the rule was changed back, which meant the return of freshman teams and only three years of varsity eligibility.

Tingle, a 6'3" forward, played from 1944 to 1947, starting as a freshman on the 1943–44 "Wildkittens" team that had a 19–2 record. He averaged 8.4 points per game that season, with a high of 22 against Fort Knox. As a sophomore, he upped his average to 11.5 while helping lead that team to a runner-up finish in the NCAA Tournament. With the arrival of standout freshmen Beard and Jones in 1945, Tingle's scoring dipped to 9.2 on that NIT championship team. In his final season, he continued to give solid performances although his scoring output dropped from previous years. Still, his efforts were good enough to earn first-team recognition on the All-SEC and All-SEC Tournament squads.

As has already been documented multiple times in these pages, Jones was a member of the Fabulous Five, a two-time NCAA champ, an NIT champ, an Olympic gold medal winner, and a superb football player. There really wasn't much he couldn't do. Oh, almost forgot. He also played baseball at UK.

Beard, like Jones, has already garnered his share of ink in this book. Everything stated above regarding Jones can be restated for Beard, even the mention of football. Not many people realize it, but as a freshman, Beard was a starting halfback on UK's football team. But his gridiron career ended when he suffered a separated shoulder during the third game of the season. After that, deciding he was too small for football, Beard concentrated all his efforts on basketball. Oh, almost forgot. He also played baseball at UK.

A couple of things about Beard that deserve mentioning. After all, he's still the yardstick by which every UK guard is measured. When Bobby Knight was coaching at Indiana, someone asked him how he thought UK's Fabulous Five would have stacked up against Indiana's undefeated 1976 team. Knight said it would be no contest, that IU would win easily. However, he went on to say that Beard was the one player on that UK team who would have given IU trouble.

Finally, Sean Woods, when seeing a photo of Beard in a book, asked Wah Wah Jones who was better, Beard or Bob Cousy. Without any hesitation, Wah Wah said Beard was clearly the superior player.

7. Jim King, Mel Brewer, Walter Johnson, Jim Goforth, and Ken England. The only reason we have freedom in this county is because many died to secure it and many others have died to defend and keep it. These five Wildcats went to war and, sadly, would not return home. If you really want to name UK's all-time starting five, here are the players you should pencil in.

Adolph Rupp with Wah Wah Jones, Jack Tingle, Joe Holland, Ralph Beard, and Kenny Rollins.
Photo courtesy of University of Kentucky Athletics.

Of the five, Goforth was the oldest, earning his three letters between 1935 and 1937. Two of the three UK teams he was on won the SEC title.

As a soldier, Goforth was awarded the Bronze Star and the Silver Star. The order awarding him the Silver Star (posthumously) read as follows:

"With his commanding officer a casualty during a heavy fire fight with the Japanese on 16 June, First Lieutenant Goforth promptly assumed command and, immediately reorganized his men under the enemy's concentrated barrages, skillfully led them in a brilliantly executed attack. Continuing his same daring tactics, he directed his company in pressing home a successful strike against Hill 500 on 20 June and, on 22 June again faced fierce hostile resistance to lead his assault units in wiping out a heavily fortified enemy pocket, killing a large number of Japanese troops before he himself was mortally wounded."

King lettered from 1940 to 1942, and while he wasn't a great player, he was a good one. He averaged 3.9 points as a sophomore, then was the team's leading scorer the following year with an average of 6.0. He was an All-SEC and an All-SEC Tournament pick in 1941.

Although King didn't put up big numbers as a sophomore in 1939–40, he was an important cog in the machine. When he and Lee Huber were sidelined by the flu bug, the Wildcats lost to Alabama, 36–32, and Vanderbilt, 40–32. Proof of just how valuable those two were to the team came in the rematch against Alabama. With them in the lineup, UK won easily, 46–18.

King was outstanding in the 1941 SEC tourney, hitting for 12 in a win over Ole Miss and 15 against Tulane.

As a senior, King was used primarily as a backup to Brewer at the center position, but once again he came up big in the SEC tourney, coming off the bench to power the Wildcats to a come-from-behind 40–31 semifinal win over Auburn. With the game tied at 28–28, King scored six points during a 10–0 run that put the Wildcats on top for good. For his efforts, King was again named to the All-SEC Tournament team.

Brewer, a Wildcat from 1941 to 1943, was probably the best player of the group. A post player, he was a three-year starter who averaged 5.1 points as a sophomore, 7.0 as a junior, and 8.3 as a senior. From his first game until his last, Brewer was a model of consistency.

Brewer's best game as a sophomore came when he scored 14 in a win over Alabama. As a junior, Brewer had a career-best 20-point effort against Georgia Tech. In his final season, Brewer's output was hampered by an injured arm that sidelined him for several games. He did play well in the SEC tourney, scoring 11 against Mississippi State and a team-high 10 points in a 33–30 loss to Tennessee in the title game. Brewer was named to the All-SEC and All-SEC Tournament teams in 1943.

England was at UK for two seasons— 1941–42—before leaving school to join the war effort. England, a guard, played sparingly as a sophomore, then alternated between starting and coming off the bench during his second season, which turned out to be his last.

He averaged 4.9 points per game that year. His key contribution came in the SEC tourney championship game against Alabama. In that heart-stopper, England was the hero, coming off the bench to rack up 13 points in a 36–34 victory. His two late free throws sealed the win for UK.

For his heroic efforts in the war, England was awarded the Bronze Star and the Silver Star. When England was posthumously awarded his Silver Star, the order read:

"For gallantry in action on 14 April 1945, near Castel d'Aiano, Italy. In the initial assault of the final offensive in Italy, Captain ENGLAND commanded a company of heavy weapons. Though his normal position was with the battalion commander, he risked his life to personally lead his men forward to ensure close support of rifle companies. Although the area was heavily mined and under constant artillery, mortar and small arms fire, he pressed forward at the head of his unit until he was fatally wounded by an exploding mine. Without thought for himself, he directed that someone take the morphine syrettes he carried to administer comfort to other of his men who were wounded. His gallant leadership and courage under fire, far beyond the call of his regular duties, will always be an inspiration to all who witnessed his heroic actions, and Captain ENGLAND has earned undying fame in keeping with the finest traditions of the United States Army."

Johnson earned one letter as a member of that 1943–44 "Wildkittens" team. He scored 74 points that season, hitting for a team-leading 15 points in a 55–54 win over Notre Dame and 13 points in a win over Indiana.

Forget about points, rebounds, assists, or All-America honors. No UK players are greater, or stand taller, than these five.

8. Harry Lancaster. Yes, Lancaster, Adolph Rupp's long-time assistant coach, was Georgetown (Kentucky) College's leading scorer in that 1930 contest. Lancaster accounted for 10 of his team's points in that 67–19 UK massacre.

In 1946, Lancaster accepted the job as Rupp's assistant coach, replacing ex-Wildcat All-American Paul McBrayer, who, following a stint in the military, returned to UK but wasn't rehired by Rupp. Some have speculated that Rupp may have considered McBrayer, an excellent tactician, recruiter, and teacher of fundamentals, as a potential threat to his job. McBrayer went on to become a highly successful coach and athletics director at Eastern Kentucky University.

As an assistant beginning in 1946, Lancaster was at Rupp's side when the Wildcats captured four NCAA championships. In addition, Lancaster served as UK baseball coach for sixteen seasons. He was also a physical education instructor.

In 1969, Lancaster was named UK's athletics director, meaning he was now Rupp's boss. This had to be an uncomfortable situation for the two men, who had always been extremely close. That changed when Lancaster became the man in charge. Things got so bad that they didn't speak with each other until 1977, when Rupp was in the hospital, dying of cancer.

As Lancaster recounted to Cawood Ledford, the final straw came when he overheard Rupp making some disparaging remarks about something to do with the athletics department. Lancaster ignored it for as long as he could, but finally called Rupp in and said, "When I was your assistant, I was very loyal to you, but now I'm your boss and I expect you to be loyal to me."

Rupp had a reputation for being a really tough guy—and to be sure, many of his players were terrified of him—but the reality is he wasn't tough. Not physically tough, anyway. Rupp's chief weapon was that sharp tongue of his, which could by turns be either sarcastic, witty, cutting, or acerbic.

Conversely, Lancaster was a genuinely tough dude. He'd knock you on your keister without giving it much thought. He wasn't a guy who would back down from a fight.

During the 1953–54 season, the Wildcats hit the road for a game against St. Louis. To say it was a wild game is putting it mildly. UK's Lou Tsioropoulos was nearly involved in a brawl, and an overly exuberant St. Louis fan took a swing at athletics director Bernie Shively.

But the real action happened at the end of the game when Lancaster slugged Pat Hickey, son of St. Louis coach Ed Hickey, for firing the timer's pistol too close to his leg. Lancaster wasn't about to tolerate that nonsense.

Here's another terrific story Cawood Ledford told that really demonstrates the difference between Rupp's perceived "tough guy" reputation and Lancaster's real one.

During a game at Tennessee, when UK was heading for the locker room at halftime, a slightly inebriated Volunteer fan cornered Rupp, waved his finger at him, and threatened bodily harm. Almost immediately, Tennessee security personnel pulled the guy away from Rupp, who then proceeded to the locker room.

After the game, which the Wildcats easily won, Rupp, his assistant coaches, Cawood, other broadcasters, and various UK big shots were in Rupp's hotel room for a postgame drink. This was typical back in those days. Beer would be iced down in the bathtub, and there would be the harder stuff for those who preferred that as an after-game tonic.

Anyway, they were all in the room when suddenly there was this loud banging on the hotel door. Along with the banging, the guy on the outside was yelling and screaming at the top of his lungs.

Now here's where the story gets really funny, because there are two distinctly different versions of what happened.

In Rupp's retelling, hearing the knock and recognizing the voice outside to be coming from the same guy who accosted him in the hallway at halftime (how he knew that is anyone's guess), he went to the door opened it, "doubled up my fist, took one swing and knocked that gentleman out cold."

A great story, only it didn't quite happen that way. According to Cawood, everything about the tale is accurate up until . . . Harry Lancaster opened the door, socked the loudmouth on the chin, and sent him into sleepsville.

Rupp wasn't the pugilist, Lancaster was.

9. Dan Issel, Frank Ramsey, Cliff Hagan, and Johnny Cox. These four, each an All-American, are UK's only career "double-double" Wildcats of all time. In addition to their rebound totals, each one of these guys scored more than 1,000 points.

The 6'9" Issel owns the distinction of being UK's all-time leader in both categories, scoring 2,138 points while yanking down 1,078 rebounds. That computes to career averages of 25.8 points and 13.0 rebounds per contest.

The big surprise on this list is Ramsey, who, at 6'3", was primarily a guard. On offense, Ramsey was a slasher, a driver to the bucket. And he was also a superb defender. As much as anything, though, Ramsey was a big-game guy, one who had a knack for performing well against the better opponents.

As Adolph Rupp once noted, "If we win by 30, he'll get you three points, but if we win by three, he'll have 30."

For his career, Ramsey scored 1,344 points (14.8) and had 1,038 rebounds (11.4).

Hagan, at 6'4", was a natural forward who was asked to operate out of the pivot position his final two seasons. In the 1951–52 campaign, he handled that spot because Bill Spivey was not allowed to play. During his final season, 1953–54, Hagan was the team's center on offense, with 6'5" teammate Lou Tsioropoulos usually defending against the opponent's biggest player.

Despite only playing in 77 games, Hagan scored 1,475 points (19.2) and grabbed 1,035 rebounds (13.4).

Cox, also 6'4", came to UK from Hazard and made an immediate impact, leading the team in scoring as a sophomore in 1956–57 with an average of 19.4 points per game. He averaged 14.9 on the 1958 NCAA championship team, then came back to score at a 17.9 clip as a senior.

As a Wildcat, Cox scored 1,461 points (17.4) and had 1,004 rebounds (12.0).

Four other Wildcats had a career rebounding average in double figures, although none cracked the 1,000-rebound mark. Bob Burrow averaged 16.1 rebounds during his two seasons at UK, while Cotton Nash averaged 12.3 rebounds in his career.

The final two only stayed at UK for one season, and both players averaged 10.4 rebounds per game—Anthony Davis in 2011–12 and Julius Randle in 2013-14.

10. Patrick Patterson. Somehow it seems proper and fitting that this classy Wildcat initiated the John Calipari Era by scoring on a tip-in 16 seconds into the season opener against Morehead State University. In this game, which UK won 75–59, Patterson finished with 20 points and 12 rebounds.

Patterson spent his first two seasons playing for Billy Gillispie, and although the Wildcats were only so-so, Patterson generally played at a very high level. When Gillispie was given his walking papers and Calipari agreed to take the job, the betting money said Patterson would head off to the NBA. That line of speculation was fueled by the influx of high-caliber talent Calipari was bringing to the UK campus, a group that included John Wall, DeMarcus Cousins, Eric Bledsoe, and Daniel Orton.

The prevailing theory was that Patterson, having been the go-to guy for two seasons, would have no desire to take a backseat to the newcomers, Wall and Cousins in particular. But those betting against Patterson's return didn't know the man.

Patterson did return and he did take a backseat to the more flamboyant Wall and the moody man-child Cousins. And he never once complained. That team, Calipari's first, had a record of 35–3, and Patterson's presence was a big reason why. He was a team leader who provided steadiness to his younger cohorts as the long season wore on. It also didn't hurt that

Patrick Patterson was one of the classiest Wildcats ever.
Photo courtesy of University of Kentucky Athletics.

his on-court performances were consistently excellent.

Even with all that offensive firepower on the team, Patterson still managed to average 14.3 points per game.

11. Hairpins. After always wearing a brown suit for every game, this was perhaps Adolph Rupp's most famous superstition. He would look for them on the ground as he headed from his car to Memorial Coliseum prior to each home game. Same thing on the road. When leaving the hotel or when walking toward the gym, Rupp would be on the lookout for those hairpins. Finding one was considered a sign of good luck.

Sometimes his assistant coaches would plant a few along the pathway in order to boost Rupp's spirits. Vernon Hatton once said that prior to one game, the players tossed several handfuls along the way. When Rupp found them he told his players, "I think we're going to have great luck tonight."

Rupp's other notorious superstitions included:
- He and his assistant coaches always wore starched khaki shirts and trousers for each practice session.
- When traveling to a road game, he would get on the bus and without looking around, he'd say, "Kick 'er, doc" and the bus took off, once leaving Mike Pratt behind. Joe B. Hall had to go back and get him.

- When the Wildcats were playing in a tournament and won the first game, he would go back to the hotel room and wash his socks.
- He always carried a buckeye, a rabbit's foot, and a four-leaf clover in his pocket.
- His wife, Esther, always fed him the same meal prior to home games—two eggs, bacon, and a slice of lightly buttered toast.

Once, when a former player asked Rupp if he was a superstitious person, Rupp replied, "No, I learned a long time ago that it's bad luck to be superstitious."

12. Jascha Heifetz. A child prodigy who gave his first public performance at age seven, Heifetz was born in Wilno, Poland (now Vilnius, Lithuania), and had a career that spanned much of the twentieth century.

   Heifetz is generally regarded as one of the finest violinists of modern times. After giving a gloriously received concert at Carnegie Hall, the *New York Times* said he was "perhaps the greatest violinist of all time."

   Simply stated: Heifetz was a genius at what he did.

   Of course, none of those accolades meant all that much to Adolph Rupp, who considered himself to be a genius when it came to coaching basketball. And, like Heifetz, Rupp had the credentials to back it up.

   While Rupp may have appreciated Heifetz's skill with the violin, that appreciation certainly didn't extend to the great musician—or anyone else for that matter—getting in the way of Kentucky basketball. And that's exactly what happened.

During one of his many tours, Heifetz scheduled a concert to be played in Lexington. That meant Memorial Coliseum, a venue known to have excellent acoustics. A venue also known as the practice home for the Kentucky Wildcats.

Naturally, prior to the concert, Heifetz, a true professional, wanted to make himself familiar with the place where he was going to perform. Most important of all, he wanted to check out the sound system to make sure it was up to his standards. The only way he could do that was to go into Memorial Coliseum on the afternoon of the concert and play the violin. Also, while he was doing that, chairs had to be placed on the basketball court to accommodate all the spectators.

On the day before the concert, Rupp was informed about what was happening, and that he would have to move practice to the old Alumni Gym down the street. Rupp was appalled, incensed that *anyone*, even the world's greatest violinist, could possibly be so important that the Kentucky Wildcats had to be relocated in order to practice basketball.

The UK big shots tried to placate Rupp but he wasn't buying it for a second.

"If he misses one note during that performance, there won't be a single person in the audience who notices it," Rupp argued. "But if one of my boys misses a free throw, everyone in the coliseum will know it."

Rupp was probably correct, but practice was moved and Heifetz gave his concert in Memorial Coliseum.

13. Paul Noel. This is another one of those scratch-your-noggin answers that can't help but leave you shaking your head in amazement. Of all the many Wildcats superstars, the first one to be on an NBA championship team is a guy who scored all of 84 points during his one-year UK career.

But before passing judgment, it might be best to hear all the facts about a player Ralph Beard said was "one heck of a basketball player, and I mean one of the best."

The 6'4" Noel, from Midway, Kentucky, had been an outstanding prep player before enrolling at UK in 1942. In his only season, he was never a starter, but he did come off the bench to give several good performances. In a 59–30 romp past Georgia in the SEC Tournament, Noel was the leading scorer with 16 points. In semifinal action against Mississippi State, a key bucket by Noel ignited a run that triggered a 52–43 come-from-behind win.

At the end of the season, Noel was forced to drop out of school when his father, a tenant farmer, became too ill to take care of the place. Noel left school to help out with things at the farm.

Several years later, Western Kentucky University coach Ed Diddle asked Noel if he would be interested in trying out for the New York Knicks in the Basketball Association of America. Diddle, who coached Noel in the Kentucky-Indiana High School All-Star Game, knew some of the people with the Knicks and they asked him if he knew anyone in the area who could play. Diddle asked Noel, who agreed to try out for the team.

Noel spent three seasons with the Knicks (1947–48 to 1949–50) and two with the Rochester Royals (1950–51 to 1951–52). In all, he totaled 661 points.

The 1951 Royals were crowned NBA champs.

Noel would later go on to become mayor of Versailles, Kentucky.

After Noel, twelve other Wildcats have been on NBA championship teams, topped by Frank Ramsey, who helped the Boston Celtics win seven titles. Lou Tsioropoulos, Ramsey's teammate at UK and Boston, was on Celtics teams that won it in 1957 and 1959. The other multiple winner is Pat Riley, who won one as a player for the Los Angeles Lakers, four more as their coach, and one with the Miami Heat.

Other NBA champs include Cliff Hagan (St. Louis, 1958), Larry Steele (Portland, 1977), Kevin Grevey (Washington, 1978), Rick Robey (Boston, 1981), Tayshaun Prince (Detroit, 2004), Nazr Mohammed (San Antonio, 2005),

Derek Anderson (Miami, 2006), Antoine Walker (Miami, 2006) and Rajon Rondo (Boston, 2008).

14. **C. M. Newton.** Although Newton was a good basketball player, he, like many others, just happened to show up at UK when the talent pool was rich and deep. Because he had to go up against guys like Bill Spivey, Cliff Hagan, and Frank Ramsey, Newton didn't get the playing time he surely would have gotten had he attended most other colleges. Another factor that kept Newton nailed to the bench was Adolph Rupp's tendency to stick with his starting five for most of the game.

Newton had been a three-sport standout at Fort Lauderdale (Florida) High School, earning All-State honors in baseball, basketball, and football. He helped lead the Flying L's to state championships in baseball and basketball.

At UK, Newton, a pitcher, had far more success on the baseball diamond than he did on the basketball court. His strong arm helped the Wildcats make it to the NCAA Tournament.

After graduating, he signed a $10,000 contract with the New York Yankees, playing in their organization before going into the Air Force. That stint in the military forced him to make a career decision upon being discharged—stick with baseball or get into coaching full-time.

"If I wanted to go back to Transylvania and be the head coach, I had to give up baseball,"

Newton said. "We had our first child, and it was very difficult to take a one-year-old on the minor league baseball (circuit). And the fact that I came out of the war and had not moved up in the organization made me decide that my best option would be go to another route."

All that decision did was lead to a Hall of Fame career as a coach, teacher, administrator, athletic director, and league commissioner. A very sound decision, wouldn't you agree?

15. Larry Boeck. These are waters we've already dipped into on several occasions so you know the basic facts. The 1953–54 team, which had a perfect 25–0 record, was then—and remains so today—one of the four or five greatest Wildcat teams in school history. This was the bunch that crushed opponents, winning their games by an average margin of 27.2 points.

Leaders on the powerful club were fifth-year seniors Cliff Hagan, Frank Ramsey, and Lou Tsioropoulos, or "The Big Three" as they have come to be known. It was this team that had very little trouble beating La Salle, which would go on to capture the NCAA title.

Everything was going great for this team until January 25, 1954, when Boeck, who covered UK for the Louisville *Courier-Journal*, broke the story that the three Wildcat standouts were not eligible to participate in the NCAA Tournament.

As you might expect, this revelation caused a big stink among UK fans, most of whom considered Boeck to be nothing less than a traitorous villain. Hagan later told Cawood Ledford that Boeck and UK assistant coach Harry Lancaster got into a fistfight because of what had transpired.

Whether or not that fight took place is uncertain. But what's not uncertain is the outcome—an unbeaten UK team, one that in all probability would have won the NCAA tourney, had to watch from the sidelines while La Salle took home the heavy hardware.

As for Boeck, after spending twenty-five years with the *Courier-Journal*, he left the paper and worked in athletic community relations at the University of Louisville.

5

FINAL SCORE

(Answers begin on Page 183)

OK, so how did you do? Maybe not quite as well as you figured, right? Well, in fairness, some of those questions went way beyond the trivia stage. No one should have to turn to Google or Wikipedia to answer a trivia question. Concerning those really difficult ones, hopefully while searching for answers, you learned something about UK basketball that you didn't know, and had some fun along the way.

Just to show you how generous I am, here are five bonus questions that might help you raise your score.

1. Name the "Super Frosh" who came to UK in 1971.

2. What Wildcat player is generally considered the most important post-probation recruit?

3. Name the three players who came to UK from Union County High School in the 1970s.

4. Which Wildcat canned two free throws with less than a second remaining to beat Louisville in the 2004–05 season?

5. Cawood Ledford once called what celebrated broadcaster "a jerk" during one of his TV commentaries?

FINAL SCORE ANSWERS

1.   Jimmy Dan Conner, Kevin Grevey, Mike Flynn, Steve Lochmueller, Bob Guyette, Jerry Hale, and G. J. Smith. This highly regarded group had a real roller-coaster ride during their time at UK. As sophomores, they helped Joe B. Hall's first team finish with a 20–8 record.

    However, the next season, when expectations were high, the best the Wildcats could do was a 13–13 record. They redeemed themselves as seniors by guiding the Cats to the NCAA championship game, where they were upended by UCLA 92–85 in John Wooden's swan song to college hoops. Along the way, those Wildcats pulled off one of UK's greatest victories, edging unbeaten Indiana 92–90 in the Mideast Regional final.

2.   Jamal Mashburn. When Rick Pitino took over at UK, he inherited a somewhat depleted roster. Most of the big-name players departed

Jamal Mashburn with Bill Keightley, UK's long-time equipment manager.
Photo courtesy of David Coyle.

UK after the scandal hit. What Pitino was left with was a group of young players, mostly in-state kids, who were long on energy, enthusiasm, courage, and had a terrific understanding of the game, but were somewhat short when it came to natural ability and athleticism. Despite those limitations, it was this group of gutsy guys who helped guide Pitino's first team to a surprising 14–14 record.

But what Pitino needed in order for his teams to play at a much higher level was a superstar. Getting one wasn't easy at that time. Opposing coaches were warning potential recruits to steer clear of Kentucky, that UK was on probation and not eligible to play in the NCAA tourney or appear on television, and that things were in such turmoil that it might takes years before the basketball program got back on sound footing.

Despite the negative talk, Pitino was able to lure Mashburn to UK, and it was on his shoulders that the Wildcats reclaimed the glory that once was.

Mashburn, a New York native, was an all-around talent, a superb athlete, and a skilled basketball player. His impact was immediate. As a freshman, he averaged 12.9 points on a team that finished with a 22–6 record. In his final two seasons, his scoring averages were 21.3 and 21.0. Those teams had won-loss records of 29–7 and 30–4, respectively.

Wildcat basketball was off and running, thanks to Mashburn's willingness to buck the odds and sign with UK during those dark days.

3. Larry Johnson, Dwane Casey, and Freddie Cowan. All three were standouts performers for the small school located in Morganfield, Kentucky. Johnson, a 1972 graduate, arrived at UK first, followed by Casey (1975), and Cowan (1976).

Johnson, a 6'3" guard, had an excellent career at UK, scoring 850 points, grabbing 390 rebounds, and handing out 319 assists. He played a key role in the 1976 team's NIT championship run, knocking down a last-second jumper to lift UK past Providence 79–78, and then coming through with 16 points in the 71–67 title-game win over UNCC.

Cowan, a slender 6'8" forward/center, also acquitted himself well during his days at UK, finishing with 975 points and 489 rebounds. His career-best effort was a 27-point, nine-rebound outing against LSU.

Casey was never a starter, but he did play a significant role in the 1977–78 team's NCAA tourney opener against Florida State. With his team trailing 39–32 after a lackluster first half, UK coach Joe B. Hall made the daring decision to bench Jack Givens, Rick Robey, and Truman Claytor at the start of the second half. Casey was one of the replacements, and thanks to their energy and inspiration, the Cats came back to win 85–76.

Two weeks later, the Wildcats beat Duke to capture the NCAA championship.

4. Patrick Sparks. Following a UK timeout with 4.8 seconds remaining and Louisville in front 58–57, Sparks inbounded the ball, took a quick return pass, did a pump fake, then went airborne for his three-point attempt, drawing a foul on Ellis Myles as the horn sounded.

While the officials got together to check the instant replay to see if time had expired before the foul was committed, veteran TV analyst Billy Packer argued that it was all moot, that Sparks had traveled before taking the shot.

The officials finally decided that Sparks would be awarded three free tosses, and that six-tenths of a second should be put back on the clock. With a hostile Freedom Hall crowd doing everything possible to rattle his nerves, Sparks stepped to the charity stripe and calmly sank all three freebies to give the Cats an improbable 60–58 rise-from-the-grave victory.

Sparks finished the game with 25 points.

5. Dick Vitale. Yes, it was Dickie V who earned Cawood's public scorn for comments Vitale made during the UK-Duke game at the 1988 Tip-off Classic. At some point in the telecast, Vitale said Eddie Sutton should resign as head coach for the good of the program.

This happened during UK's season opener, and Cawood felt the timing of Vitale's statement was misguided. Cawood also thought that it was wrong for Vitale to call for Sutton's resignation when none of the allegations against him had been proven.

So, Cawood began his nightly TV commentary by saying, "Dick Vitale is a jerk."

"I had always liked Vitale," Cawood wrote in his autobiography, "but I thought he had shown a total disregard for fairness, and I felt I had to say that."

Cawood went on to write that he and Dickie V patched up their differences and became friends again.

And as everyone knows, Sutton did resign at the end of the 1988–89 season.

About the Author

Tom Wallace is a former award-winning sportswriter who covered UK basketball while working for legendary broadcaster Cawood Ledford and as a columnist for *The Cats' Pause*. He is the author of several sports-related books, including the highly successful *University of Kentucky Basketball Encyclopedia*, now out in its fourth edition. He has also written books with former Wildcats Travis Ford and Jeff Sheppard.

David Coyle

As a freelance writer, Tom has written seven mystery/thriller novels, the most recent being *The Poker Game*. His other novels include *The Fire of Heaven, The List, Gnosis, Heirs of Cain, The Devil's Racket,* and *What Matters Blood.*

In 2010, Tom's novel, *Gnosis*, won the prestigious Claymore Award at the Killer Nashville Writers' Conference. *Gnosis* would go on to become one of the most downloaded e-books on Amazon in 2013. In 2007, *The Devil's Racket* also took home a top prize, capturing the Mystery Novel Award.

A graduate of Western Kentucky University's outstanding journalism department, Tom spent many years as a successful sportswriter. From 1983 to 1986, he served as sports editor for the *Gleaner* in Henderson, Kentucky, where he was twice honored by the Kentucky Press Association for writing the best sports story in the state.

Tom, a Vietnam vet, lives in Lexington. He is a member of Mystery Writers of America. His Web site is www.tomwallacenovels.com.